Until One Has Loved an Animal

Until One Has Loved an Animal

How Pets Affected One Vet's Soul

Mildred A. Drost, DVM

iUniverse, Inc.
Bloomington

Until One Has Loved an Animal
How Pets Affected One Vet's Soul

iUniverse books may be ordered through booksellers or by contacting:

iUniverse
1663 Liberty Drive
Bloomington, IN 47403
www.iuniverse.com
1-800-Authors (1-800-288-4677)

Because of the dynamic nature of the Internet, any web addresses or links contained in this book may have changed since publication and may no longer be valid. The views expressed in this work are solely those of the author and do not necessarily reflect the views of the publisher, and the publisher hereby disclaims any responsibility for them.

Any people depicted in stock imagery provided by Thinkstock are models, and such images are being used for illustrative purposes only.

Certain stock imagery © Thinkstock.

ISBN: 978-1-4759-6082-2 (sc)
ISBN: 978-1-4759-6083-9 (hc)
ISBN: 978-1-4759-6084-6 (e)

Library of Congress Control Number: 2012921151

Printed in the United States of America

iUniverse rev. date: 01/04/2013

This book is dedicated to all those who strive to prevent abuse, neglect, and cruel acts toward our animals. It's for those who do their best to rescue, assist, treat, and rehome our strays. It's for those who champion respect and kindness toward (and honourable treatment of) all pets, livestock, and wildlife.

It is also dedicated to all of our animal friends—past, present, and future!

Until one has loved an animal, a part of one's soul remains unawakened.

Anatole France, 1844–1924

Contents

Introduction 1

Chapter 1— On-Call Quill Dogs. 5

Chapter 2—Those Malamutes. 13

Chapter 3— The Cost of Calls. 27

Chapter 4— Freeman and Me 35

Chapter 5—Don't Fence Me In. 47

Chapter 6— Humour Helps 55

Chapter 7—Euthanasia: The "Good" Death 63

Chapter 8— The Games People Play 71

Chapter 9—DunRoamin' 74

Chapter 10—Buddy 81

Chapter 11—The Pups, More or Less 86

Chapter 12—Those Darn Cats 92

Chapter 13—The Diva 97

Chapter 14—When Harry Met Mil 103

Chapter 15—Sunday Mornings, Sayin' "Down" 108

Chapter 16—Larry the Cat. 113

Chapter 17—It Can Be Done; It's Easy. 117

Chapter 18—Bedtime. 124

Chapter 19—Conversations 129

Afterword 137

Introduction

Veterinary medicine is a second career for me. I started out as a nurse in the human health-care system. I do not regret my decision to leave my job as a registered nurse to return to university and become a veterinarian. I enjoyed the 14 years that I worked as an intensive care and emergency room nurse and the experiences that I had in that field. My heart, though, has always been in the animal world. Animals have always been my favourite topic—and they've formed the basis of my career, hobbies, and main interests in life. As my confidence as a nurse grew, I started to think that I might want to do more and that maybe I could become a doctor. Then, with that idea firmly entrenched in my head, I knew which type of doctor I wanted to be.

Throughout my career as a vet, I have been able to enjoy and experience the absolute thrill of helping other species in need while enjoying the uniqueness of their behaviours. Their obvious intelligence and goodness is evident in every single case. Along the way, I have also met some truly amazing people.

When I opened my own practice, I was amazed by the questions that I was asked. "Do they feel pain like we do?" (Yes!) "If he is in pain, why isn't he yelping?" (He's stoic, like some people.) "Do they get cold like we do?" (You bet! And hungry and thirsty and bored and frightened and lonely!) I was also amazed—horrified, actually—by the too-frequent requests to *euthanize* healthy pets because their owners thought it convenient to do so. I heard all sorts of comments: "We're going on vacation"; "He sheds"; "He pulls me on the leash"; "The litter box stinks"; "I don't have time for him." I had never before been required to take complete control of practice policymaking, and I had never been a leader, a mover and shaker. Still, I needed to be able to sleep at night. My practice policies needed to be consistent with the demands of my conscience. This sense of responsibility—and my great capacity for guilt—was the root of the attitude that developed at the clinic. Many people were annoyed with these policies; others celebrated them.

My first official policy stated that we would not put down normal, healthy animals. I knew that if I (as a veterinarian) did not at least question these requests and advocate for the animals, nobody would. To comply with every request without question implied that I was in agreement with the practice of killing healthy pets. Taken further, it might seem like I found no fault with the "throwaway pet" mentality. That statement could not be further from the truth.

Second, I could not *euthanize* the poor, homeless waifs found on the street or in the woods that had been so obviously struggling for extended periods to survive. Who am I to take a starving, injured cat who has struggled for so long under such formidable adversity and end its life—especially when some antibiotics, food, and warm shelter were all he needed? Surely I could spare a few dollars to assist this heroic struggle?

This, then, became the basis for the philosophy and methodology of managing what was often a heartbreaking situation. Thankfully,

I have found others who subscribe to the same beliefs. My first associate, Shannon; my sister, Martha; and many really wonderful people agree with these practices—without them, DunRoamin' Stray and Rescue Inc. would not exist. This rescue for injured, sick, or starving stray pets evolved from efforts to assist stray animals that had no options because they had been discarded. These were the animals with which the shelter system was unable to cope due to their medical requirements and the resulting costs. It started as a way to give back to the weak, to promote awareness about their plight in a way that showed respect for their lives, and to care for them. The number of animals in need of help in our rural community necessitated that an entire group of people work on their behalf. When the stray pets come to us, we say that they are all "DunRoamin'."

Many of the stories presented in this book concentrate more on the behaviours, attitudes, and attributes of my patients and pets rather than their guardians or owners. This was done because they have been my inspiration and source of enjoyment and fascination. When I was a small child, my grandparents and my father began pointing out the responses of animals (cows, cats, dogs, chickens) to different situations and the animals' problem-solving abilities. I have always, since then, felt that there was some thought and decision-making involved in their responses. As far back as I can remember, I have disagreed with the statements that animals respond only by instinct, not with intelligence. They are as individual as we are. I ascribe feelings, emotions, intelligence, and personal preferences to each animal. I believe that very strongly. These are very sentient creatures. We as a society must learn to accept that. These stories are intended to open the reader's mind to the possibility that there is much more to our animal companions' emotional and internal lives than is widely accepted—and to add credence to the beliefs of those who already know this.

Yes, I pay my bills and support myself as a veterinarian, but the main rewards of this job are not financial. During my training, internship, and practice, I have had so many amazing experiences. I have held a bald eagle in my hands! I have petted live musk oxen! I have helped treat an Arctic wolf! I have peered rather closely at a huge boa constrictor! I have held a peregrine falcon and released him into the wild! I have been greeted with a "high five" by a ten-week-old black lab, sitting on my exam table! I have taken blood samples from a seal! I have been honoured to meet people who go out of their way to help abandoned, lost, or injured pets—and those who spend much of their time trying to educate people so that they provide better care to their animals! I have treated a moose with a sore foot and a very large pot-bellied pig whose bout with constipation effectively removed the *new* smell from my clinic! I have scars from bites by dogs smaller than most cats! I have had my heart melted by injured, stray tomcats lying in my arms, purring, and patting my face with their paws! I have moved dogs that were hit by cars, knowing that it must cause great pain (and they didn't try to bite me)! I have met burly and gruff policemen at the clinic door with half-frozen, stray cats tucked into their own down jackets to provide them with warmth! I have held a crow-sized pileated woodpecker in my hands and watched him fly away, recovered from his brush with death! I have met a group of the most dedicated and compassionate volunteer animal caretakers ever to be assembled! I have become part of DunRoamin'!

Through my profession, I have had the honour of meeting many absolutely terrific beings—human, canine, feline, and wild. I have had hilarious interludes. I have been badly shocked and horrified. I have seen miracles! I have met miracles! I have experienced miracles! I have become part of the best career in the world. I am a veterinarian.

Chapter 1—On-Call Quill Dogs

"There!" I sighed as I pulled what seemed like the one millionth porcupine quill from the huge male Rottweiler's mouth. Blood dripped from the most recent extraction sites on his massive jaw, leaving glistening scarlet droplets on the pale, tiled floor. His muzzle extended over the end of my exam table, and all four legs protruded past the edges, streaked and smeared with drying blood. The tabletop and its three sides were an abstract painting, red on white. Footprints were evident here and there on the floor, and a decent crime scene investigator would have had no problem identifying the perpetrator. Fingerprints—and even entire handprints—could be easily lifted from the scene. The perfect prints of my shoes (Naturalizers, size 8 1/2) were in full view, and I noted that I had stepped in several of the freshest blood smears.

Although I had no experience tracking porcupines, I felt that I could say with some certainty that most of those animals were found in wet or swampy areas. My opinion was based on the repeated appearance of my "quill dog" patients: wet to the chest, feet and legs covered with black, often foul-smelling mud. The mud is memorable due to its ability to smear the light floors of my clinic and merge with the blood to create an almost purple hue. The mixture seemed to require

5

twice the normal effort to remove it from the floors, and I sighed as I recognized the signs of a protracted cleanup after the eventual discharge of the dogs.

Clumps of two-by-two cotton gauze littered the room, and multiple quills protruded from each clump. Quills are easily released from the extracting forceps by inserting the end of each quill into the gauze (after they are removed from the dog). The barbs on the business end of the quills catch on the strands in the gauze, and they remain there when the forceps are opened. Today, many, many clumps of gauze had been pierced by quills. Glancing around, I wondered fretfully which product it was that removed blood from clothing with the best results. My bloodied lab coat told a grisly but inaccurate story, and I deeply regretted wearing my favourite blue jeans to this two-quill-dogs call.

"From now on, let's leave the body piercing to the professionals," I advised the sleeping form of the mammoth dog as I slid him from the exam table and down my body to rest on the floor with just a slight thump. "Body piercing is just not what it's cracked up to be!"

Quill dogs are frequently encountered when veterinarians are on call for emergencies. The predators are disabled by their prey. The large quills protecting the slow porcupine pierce the lips, tongue, throat, hard palate, and face of the attacking dog—and often the feet, legs, and chest as the dog makes a poorly thought-out attack on what should have been an easy kill. The result is a very painful beard of sharp spines that have barbs at their ends to add an exquisite agony when extracted. The porcupine's protection is simple and elegant. It simply turns its back to its attacker and elevates its many spines (it wears a jacket of 30,000 tiny, easily detached spears, all at the ready). With its head down, it waits for the chance to strike its aggressor with its strong, spiny tail. Attempts to bite are repelled by the spines projecting from its body. Like a large grey-brown pincushion—needles pointing in reverse—it attempts to wait out its attackers. Reviled by dog owners, porcupine attacks are almost unheard of. Their game plan is avoidance. So who do we blame? Many dogs are easily repelled by the first, sharp touch, but others become spurred by the excitement of the attack and the pain—they kill the porcupine despite the terrible cost to themselves. This is the category to which I felt today's quill dogs belonged.

Carefully, I made one final check of my patient. I felt the thick black and tan skin folds of his face and jowls with my fingertips for any hint of the thin, firm, barbed spines of the dog's ill-fated prey. Next, I rechecked his massive shoulders, neck, and chest before palpating the joints of his huge front legs. His body filled much of the treatment room floor where I had placed him to recover from the anaesthetic. Trepidation lent wings to my fingers as I noted his breathing rate increase and his huge frame start to move—he was rapidly regaining consciousness. He quickly discarded the endotracheal tube that had kept his windpipe open so he could receive anaesthetic and oxygen during the procedure. He and his erstwhile companion—a large male Rottweiler mix with an aggressive and fearful attitude—had made short work of the unlucky porcupine and long work for me. Their faces initially had huge, painful beards of quills with many more in their necks, legs, and feet, but I persevered until I had removed all that I could find.

My holiday weekend had been interrupted by the call from their owner who demanded that I attend to his animals immediately. I had survived the initial meeting with the man and sifted through his various stories: "They are not my dogs"; "They both have good temperaments"; "I don't have any money, but I can't leave my poor pups to suffer"; "The biggest one is aggressive, but the smaller one will bite"; "I get paid next week"; "I can't afford that much, so I guess I'll take them home and shoot them"; and "A guy owes me some money, and I will get that before I come to pick up my dogs."

It always amazes me how perfect strangers expect to be given credit for work done on their animals (granted, this guy was far less than perfect). Often, when I ask whether customers have credit cards or whether someone else could lend them the payment, the answer is no. It always makes me think, *If no one who knows you will lend you money* ...

I dreaded the possibility that he might return without the funds to cover my fees for the entire holiday afternoon. He had offered to pay me next week too, a plan that I found suspect in view of his varying stories. Plus, I'd never met the man or his dogs before, so it would be hard to track him down if he didn't bring the money. The bottom line was that the dogs badly needed my help, and fees or not, after having seen them, I knew I couldn't ignore their plight.

The Rotty lifted his head and surveyed the floor of my treatment room with a fascinated but unfocused stare. The drugs that I had administered to relax and sedate him had done their job well. As I watched, he made several unsuccessful attempts to lever himself to his feet but he had not yet regained control of both ends of his impressive anatomy. Carefully, I plotted my escape routes in case this guy lived up to his owner's smug description of his attitude (as the other dog had).

I sensed that the other dog, the Rottweiler mix, was a fearful dog that was poorly socialized to people and different surroundings. His uncertainty about the ways of people and their motives made him afraid. Lack of experience with people (or perhaps even some experiences with bad people) frightened him, and he reacted aggressively to hide that fear—as many people do. Although this type of fear-based aggression can be overcome by committed owners and sensitive retraining, I doubted that this fellow would find help in his situation. Still, many of these dogs are comfortable in familiar surroundings and with familiar people. Knowing that I was very unlikely to form any kind of friendship with this dog in the short time we were together, I opted to do my best to reduce the stress that he was experiencing and avoid frightening him. I avoided direct eye contact, handled him minimally, and left some treats in his kennel while I attended to his friend. It was all that I could offer in these circumstances.

"Hey, Mister," I crooned to the awakening Rottweiler. "And who's a good doggy?" I was careful to keep my voice soft and low to avoid startling him. As I watched, his glazed eyes suddenly focused on my face, and he struggled again on wobbly legs to gain his footing. His stubby tail wagged that half of him and hindered his efforts to stand. A glance at his eyes told me that his attitude—at least for the moment—was far from aggressive, and I moved forward to steady him as he attempted again to stand. A huge pink tongue aimed for my face and only swift reflexes honed from years of handling dogs allowed me to escape the slimy kiss destined for my mouth.

"You're just a little kisser," I said and smiled. I relaxed to enjoy my moments with this lovable big dog whose role, I suspected, was to protect his owner's drug enterprise in the backwoods of New Brunswick.

I'd been a dog fan for years—since childhood, in fact—and I found that I liked (or at least sympathized with) every dog I'd ever met.

After spending twelve years raising and training Alaskan malamutes in conformation and obedience—and sledding recreationally—I had decided to return to university and become a veterinarian. My goal was to be able to work daily with the animals that fascinated me. And I hoped to make my little area of the world a better place in which to be a pet. There was much work to be done, but I had many allies in the area.

I wanted a nice caring home for this Rottweiler, one where he would be a loving companion to a kind, loving owner. I wanted that for all the animals that I saw, and I was inordinately pleased when I saw patients in my clinic from that kind of home. Sitting on the floor with my newest favourite dog, I reflected on the situation from which these two animals had come. Both were in good body condition and well fed. Plus, the owner was concerned enough to invest in their well-being by bringing them to me for help. I've seen what happens to unfortunate animals whose owners chose to "teach them a lesson" by leaving the quills in place for several days. I was grateful that these dogs had gotten help. Left in place, the barbed end of the quill can be pulled by its impingement on the muscle fibres as they move, and it can be gradually drawn entirely under the skin. Retained quills have been known to pierce eyes, prevent swallowing, and cause serious organ damage and major infections. In brief, the longer they are left in place, the more medical management is required—thus inflating the costs of veterinary care.

Cuddles and I now waited, his companion safely locked in a kennel for my protection and for his comfort (he truly did not appreciate my manner, bedside or otherwise). Would the owner be back? And if so, would he have the money? The best I could do for my new friend was to praise his beauty and intelligence, his protective instincts, and his value as a deterrent to home invasion. I thought that would elevate his value (and perhaps his care) to a higher level. I'd put in a good word for his companion as well, even though we had not become as close. Straining, I pushed Mr. Wonderful off my lap, ducked to avoid another wet and intimate kiss, and went to answer the clinic doorbell.

The owner had returned, and he was peeling cash from the large roll that he pulled from the pocket of his faded jeans. He glanced around the room, seemingly ignoring my instructions regarding post-anaesthetic management of the dogs and the need to monitor for hidden quills. He did focus on my praise for the beauty and value of his dogs, and he smiled slightly as I voiced my fear of approaching his house unannounced.

"Yep," he replied, "these here dogs'd die for me if I need 'em to."

"Well," I responded, "here's hoping that they don't have to. You'd never find as nice a pair again."

"No, I bet I wouldn't," he answered, seeming to view his dogs with new appreciation.

"Come on, boys," he called, and I stood back from the kennel as I released the Rotty mix to run to his owner. Surreptitiously, Mr. Snuggles and I shared a big sloppy wet kiss before he too ran from the clinic to join his family. I smiled as I watched their owner put his dogs in the cab of his truck, remembering how they had arrived: loose and dangerously unrestrained on the back of his half-ton.

After entertaining the very brief thought that I could leave the mess until tomorrow morning, I resignedly began cleaning the room. Dried blood and mud can be difficult to remove, I was again reminded, especially with tired, aching hands. Nonetheless, I persevered until it was clean enough to be acceptable for the morning clients. Fortunately, there was still no crime scene technician around to use his Luminol spray on my treatment room. My guess is that the entire room would probably fluoresce with the residue of the blood stains. Staff would do a better job tomorrow. Cleaning notwithstanding, I'd done my best for the dogs. I could only hope that their owner would too. Had I elevated their value in his eyes? I hoped so.

Chapter 2—Those Malamutes

I spent much of my free time as a child (and as an adult) with animals. After receiving my DVM degree at the age of forty, I was still somewhat in awe of my newfound responsibilities and the vast area of expertise I was assumed to have mastered. My previous efforts with my own dogs, the Alaskan malamutes, stood me in good stead in my new profession. I had learned a lot about dogs and their handling from the often-difficult northern breed.

Accustomed as I was to the civilized and obedient Border collie types on the farm, the attitude and behaviour of the independent mal was an eye-opener for me. Alaskan malamutes are the largest of the northern sled dogs, named after the Inuit Mahlemuit tribe with which they evolved. They are independent, eager to work, assertive, and stubborn. Most are friendly to all—not guard dogs. Their prey drive, willingness to fight for position in the pack, competitiveness, well-recognized sense of humour, playfulness, and sharp intelligence all evolved in harsh Arctic conditions where survival was an almost-daily concern.

With no daily survival concerns at our house, our mals turned to mischievousness, stubbornness, and any behaviour contrary to my wishes or demands. Try as I might, I could not coax from them the obedient, eager-to-please attitude of the collies. At my command to sit, their expressions would seem to say, "What for?" or "What's in it for me?" With time and an excellent obedience instructor (and tons of treats), however, I was able to convince these independent and mischievous dogs to follow some of my commands. I succeeded in qualifying several dogs for titles in obedience trials. Note that there is a reason why they are called *trials,* especially if you are training Alaskan malamutes.

They were great dogs for young energetic people because they were constantly getting into trouble, and they required frequent and strenuous exercise. It was from my efforts with them that I began my motto "A good dog is a tired dog." I still believe strongly that this is the root of many behaviour problems that my clients describe to me. Dogs were meant to move—to run, to herd, to patrol, to retrieve, to hunt, to chase, to pull, and so on. That's why, when I was younger, I decided to jog daily with a very active and intelligent (and troublesome) young male malamute named Max. It couldn't hurt me either—jogging is great exercise!

Each day, we would leave our home and jog along the road—uphill for a kilometre, until we reached a level area. We then continued our run along a farm road, away from the cattle, cats, and chickens that lived at the nearby farm. Max had made short work of the occasional hapless, free-roaming chicken that wandered into our yard in the past, and at all costs, I wanted to avoid any further displays of his hunting prowess.

It was fall, and the grain was being harvested. I had not yet mastered the effortless run to the farm road that I felt would become easier by the day. The uphill section still left me (but not Max) winded, no matter how slowly or strategically I covered that portion of my run.

Max had become used to our routine, and he knew that reaching the back of the farm meant he would be allowed to run free beside me. He loved it, and he had been so attentive on the uphill jog, never tightening the leash and behaving impeccably for the last two weeks. As a reward, I decided to show my faith in him by releasing him from the leash earlier in the run. As we ran, the farm truck that I had noticed carrying barrels of freshly harvested grain earlier in the day breezed past us, chaff flying in our faces from the draft created. Certain now that the road was safe, I released Max from his leash and continued my run. Just then, I noticed a large, reddish bird fly clumsily from the back of the truck. Realizing that an unnoticed chicken had been eating the grain spillage on the truck as it left the farm, and that it too had blown off the back of the truck to land in the nearby field, I instantly issued a *stay!* command and grabbed for the dog's collar. Too late! The opportunist had seen the chicken as soon as I did, but he had reacted even faster and was now crossing the intervening space in great leaps. Fruitlessly, I shouted a myriad of commands at the unheeding dog: "Max, come! Max, no! Max, down!" All of these commands he had responded to with crisp precision and unerring reliability not five minutes before (and for the past month during practice sessions). Before my horrified eyes, he rapidly overtook the chicken and closed his mouth over his prey. Still ignoring my gasping, shouted commands, he turned toward home and disappeared over a small hill in that direction.

Current dog training methods said that the owner should show the dog who is alpha (the boss), and that deliberate disobedience must be dealt with instantly. I believed that at the time, and despite my winded condition, I began to sprint toward home to try to save the bird and teach this recalcitrant animal that important lesson. I arrived home minutes behind Max—only to discover that he had taken his prize through a small opening in the latticework surrounding our large deck. He was holed up under the deck forty feet across at the far side. Still oblivious to my gasping, hoarsely shouted commands—and my assessment of his character—he lay glaring at me, chicken dangling lifelessly from his huge jaws.

"Max, come!" I gasped, "Max, you're bad!" I asserted, but to no avail. True to my hair colour (and face just as red), anger boiled over. This dog would *not* get the better of me! Determined, I squeezed myself through the opening used by the little jerk and crawled the forty feet through spider webs, bugs, fungi, and mosses of all descriptions. And then I went this way and that to head off the dog until, with a final lunge, I was able to grab his collar.

"Now I've got you, you rotten little thing," I muttered as I dragged his 90-pound body (100 pounds with the chicken) back toward the light of the opening. Mud and dust clung to my sweaty clothes, and I shuddered at the sensation of bugs crawling on my skin.

Fresh, clean air greeted us as I dragged him from his hiding place. Still breathless and agitated—and noting that the bird was truly dead—I continued in my attempt to redeem my superiority over this wilfully disobedient dog.

"Drop it!" I commanded in my most authoritative voice. "Max, drop it!" No way! Raised on dry kibble, he was not about to forego the fresh meat for anyone. Fastening the leash to his collar to create a more reliable restraint, I tied him to the deck rail. I had both hands free to manage the dog. One hand on the chicken and one at the juncture of his powerful jaws, I strained to loosen his grip on his prey. Just as I was about to admit defeat, I felt his grip loosen. Immediately, I increased the pressure to his jaws, and panting and swearing, I felt it release from his mouth. Tragically, as I was pulling it away, he made a small lunge and impaled part of the chicken with his powerful and long canine teeth. My momentum pulled the chicken away from him, but it left a long string of intestine hooked on his one-inch lower canine tooth. It spanned the three feet between us. Stupefied, I stared in horror at the result of our struggle. I was amazed that our relationship had come to this. With arms like noodles, I dragged Max across the yard to his kennel. Each of us was still in possession of our part of the grisly prize. Wedging him through the door of his kennel and pulling it partially closed, I placed my part of the prize on the ground outside the run and managed to lever the seven-foot remainder from his jaws before slamming closed the metal and wire door. We both stood staring at each other—he with a delighted expression in appreciation of the great romp we'd just had, and me in disbelief, covered with mud, blood, feathers, and spider webs (and feeling responsible for the chicken's death). I wondered, *Now, what did we learn from that?*

That night, as I related our experiences to my husband, Larry—who had been having a particularly hard time teaching Max to stay reliably—we discussed how we could modify his behaviour and ours to decrease the likelihood of a repeat of this episode. After much theorizing, Larry said plaintively, "You know, if he lives to be 12, I'll be 44 before he dies. And then I'll probably have to bury him three or four times, 'cause he's never stayed any place I've put him yet!"

Those malamutes were responsible for my interest in dog behaviour and training—and for my eventual graduation from the school of hard knocks. Desperation and admiration fuelled my desire to understand the seemingly indecipherable reasons for their behaviour. It was truly amazing to fly behind those dogs on the sled, the closest I would ever come to running with the wolves. Still, after carefully separating potential troublemakers on the team and keeping only the best of friends as close teammates, sometimes those very friends would erupt into a fight on the trail—apparently without provocation. Well-trained team members would suddenly fail to follow commands or dart off the trail in search of some fuzzy creature, dragging teammates along with them. I scoured every book available trying to find the answer to my problems with chronic disobedience. I had meanwhile trained my father's Border collie in basic obedience in a quarter of the time (and with a tenth of the aggravation I experienced training the mals). Was it me?

When I returned to university, it was necessary to move closer to the campus. The dogs were packed up and moved with us. We acquired yet another malamute, a pup whose show prospects in the conformation ring were nil. Although she lacked much in physical type, she more than compensated for it with her wonderful personality and her aversion to fighting.

As a 12-week-old pup, she had been outside most of the day, playing with some of the adult dogs and following Larry around the yard. As he opened the door to let her inside, she spotted me at the other side of the living room. Excitement and delight glowed in her face as she shot across the room to greet me (I had left her side a full five minutes previously). Suddenly, stopping short of my feet, she gave a mighty heave and deposited a wet mess not two inches from my stocking-clad feet. Interspersed with some undisturbed, slightly wet-looking kibbles were a sock, seven grasshoppers, and a squirrel tail. To my husband's delight—and without even moving my feet—I commented, "So that's where that sock went." You know you've been around dogs too much when …

We were still trying to show our dogs, and the youngest, Lacey (a gentle grey female) was the last to earn her obedience degree. I drove Lacey four hours to a trial one weekend when she was a year old. I knew that if I got into veterinary school, there would be no time for dog shows. I knew she was capable of getting her basic obedience degree, and I hoped to get the final two legs that weekend. Lacey loved all the dogs and activity at the show grounds. She wagged her tail and presented smiling eyes to everyone who spoke to her. She was full of fun and thoroughly enjoyed the day. That night in the motel room, I watched as she restlessly circled the room, seemingly unable to settle (even though I had brought her bed with me). Eventually, I fell asleep and was dreaming. Obviously, foremost in my mind were the dogs. In my dream, I was panicking, trapped under a load of high-performance dog food. I couldn't breathe! I couldn't move! Awakened by my struggles, I focused on a large nose touching my chin and a great grey head lying on my chest. Unused to sleeping alone, Lacey had made the best of the situation.

Even after I started vet school, those dogs were a big part of my life. We bought a cottage on a small lake in PEI, and we lived there for the four years of my training. After those four years, most of the malamutes were geriatric—with the exception of Lacey. She went with me to the college whenever she was needed for public demonstrations. The college hosted a yearly open house in which the public was invited to visit and tour the Atlantic Veterinary College. Information booths were set up in different parts of the building to encourage interest and demonstrate such areas as surgery, exotic animals, farm animals, and pets. Lacey had been invited to be at the pet's booth due to her friendly, outgoing personality and love of children. She was silver-grey with a rangy, wolfish appearance not prized by malamute breeders. As we stood greeting the children and their families, I heard a disdainful young male ask, "Raised in captivity, was she?" I understood his distaste for that, since I, too, strongly believed that wild animals should not be kept as pets. Aware of his mistake in assuming her wolfish appearance was the real thing, I hurried to explain, "This is a dog, an Alaskan malamute dog." Sheepishly, he walked away. At that time, wolves and wolf-hybrids were starting to become popular as pets. I liked that young man because he realized that wild animals do not make good, safe, or happy additions to a human family.

Throughout vet school and an internship, my eight mals gradually succumbed to age and natural causes. Eventually, I was left with only Lacey. She had seen me through pre-vet, veterinary college, and an internship at the Western College of Veterinary Medicine in Saskatoon, Saskatchewan. Now, herself geriatric, we were starting on my new life as a small animal veterinarian. Lacey's presence was still a benefit to me, both personally and professionally. Her beauty and love of people bolstered my image as a small animal veterinarian, and her friendly, self-deprecating admission to the children that she was White Fang made us memorable to the youngsters. Her complete acceptance of everyone that she met—and her complete acceptance of my moods—made life so much easier. She was always there, always seeming to say, "It'll be all right."

One of the first mals I saw as a patient had a penchant for eating indigestible and dangerous objects. He would pick them up and swallow them as fast as possible when his owner approached to avoid having them taken away. My first visit with him was as a result of his gobbling of a large cat toy that I feared would cause an intestinal obstruction. Since it had been only a short time since ingestion, I gave him some medication to induce vomiting in an effort to expel the object. After some mighty heaves, the cat toy landed on the floor. Only my lightning-quick reflexes prevented him from wolfing it down again. Two weeks later, his owner again returned to the emergency room where I was working. This time, his dog had swallowed his ski glove. After some thought, I emptied a half tube of lubricant into some cat food and told the mal not to eat it. It was gone in seconds, and I then administered the medication to bring on the vomiting. Again we successfully retrieved the lubricated object. A week after that, his frustrated owner returned immediately following the ingestion of one of his work socks. And another visit ensued a week following that to retrieve another article. The mal, his owner, and I were getting into a routine and developing a friendship. A few weeks later, the owner brought his mal in for his yearly check-up and vaccinations. Although I often hear owners say that they don't even see their own doctor every year, I like to compare this yearly visit to seeing your doctor every seven years. After all, dogs age so much faster than we do, and conditions develop and become serious issues in a much shorter amount of time. After greeting me as usual, the mal studied my face and promptly vomited his entire stomach contents at my feet—so much for conditioning!

Those malamutes were the most beautiful dogs that I had ever seen. They were intelligent (if it was to their benefit to learn), loving, and friendly (but jealous and liable to erupt into fights at the slightest provocation from another dog). As malamute guardians, we had to be constantly on our toes, aware of who was out with whom, who was harnessed next to whom, who got the first hug or treat, and so on. Even my lead dog on sledding trips was only 75 percent trustworthy, despite having two degrees in obedience and hours and hours of training in commands used for sledding. My temper would flare at his disobedience on the trail because he had demonstrated to me time and time again that he understood the commands. My attempts to race recreationally often ended in disgrace. His wilful disobedience caused my blood to boil and inspired my version of Rudyard Kipling's well-known poem, "If."

If

If you can keep your team on the trail
When all about you are losing theirs
And blaming it on you;
If you can trust your team
And leave them on a *stay*
Without worry of a fight or scuffle;
If yours will wait (because you say, "Wait")
While all other teams go off ahead
And hike when you say, "Hike"
And not before instead—and not yell
and lunge while waiting to go;

If your dogs will trot on past delectable woodland smells
With merely a glance in that direction
And work as a team, without some recalcitrant dog
Trying to mark the trail or grab some furry creature
That just passed into view;
If you can motivate your team to catch the team ahead
And, yes, pass that team
With nary so much as a growl—
And, having passed, to continue on at good speed,
Past spectators and back to the finish line
Without one dog acting like a jerk
Or mauling even one person in friendly greeting;
If you can run an entire race
Without saying even one bad word …

Then, my friend, you must be driving a team of golden retrievers
    'Cause I've never met a mal team or driver yet
  Who didn't succumb to at least one of those temptations!

Despite his love of hunting chickens, my big male, Max, was a pretty good lead dog when he wanted to be. He would work tirelessly and honestly, giving me the "running with the wolves" feeling that I loved. He was a powerhouse, pulling an unwilling team onto a new trail in response to my command. He looked at me over his shoulder in proud awareness, knowing that we were working together and leading the others into the trails we chose. Those were the days I loved, and I returned from those outings feeling so proud of Max that I could not believe my luck at having such a great dog. But he had a Mr. Hyde personality, and I could not figure out what set him off. Sometimes he was a total jerk, refusing to follow even the most simple commands. Here's how one of those trips went:

> Harness dogs. Load in van. Fasten sled on top. Drive to sledding trail. Get out. Unload sled. Open van. Pieces of foam and seat cushion cover fly through air. Note lead dog with mouthful of foam. Cuff lead dog. Tell him what sort of dog I perceive him to be. Hook dogs to sled. Note leader appears sullen. Shout, "Hike!" Sled shoots forward. Come to crossroads in trail. Shout confidently, "Straight on!" Leader turns left. Demand halt. Reinforce earlier opinion of lead dog. Drag leader back to proper trail. Shout, "Hike."
>
> Dogs take off. Come to second crossroads. Shout, "Straight on!" Leader turns left. Earlier opinion confirmed. Demand another halt. Scuffle resulting in dogs resuming run on proper trail. Come to another crossroads. Shout,

"Haw!" Leader continues straight. Grind teeth. Count to ten—twice. Manhandle leader onto trail to left. Shout, "Hike!"

Team trots forward. Trail becomes narrow path zigzagging downhill through woods. Leader opens throttle to "Race." Trees become a blur. Croon, "Easy, boy, easy" in attempt to slow leader. Leader deaf. Hang on to sled as if life depended on it. It does! Mario Andretti would be proud. Steer sled desperately. Foot slips off runner. Toe catches on exposed root of tree. Glance back to see entire sole of boot wedged under root. Resolve to buy sturdier footwear. Try to balance on one foot. Bottom of other foot cold. Top isn't bad. Try to pitch voice for proper sounding *easy* to slow dogs. Dogs don't respond to squeak. Hairpin turn ahead. Bounce brush bow of sled off unyielding cedar tree. Sharp snap of wood cracking. One foot very cold. Brush bow now in position to serve as second handle. Dogs unconcerned. Trail enters open field. Dogs settle into extended trot. Try to get breathing under control while standing on one foot. Remember all the nice things about toy poodles.

Return to van. Car stops. Occupants fascinated by dogs. Ask many questions. Query design of sled and reason for two handles. Dogs behave perfectly. No reason to cut short conversation. Pride demands standing on two feet. Finally end conversation. Foot no longer feels cold. Unharness dogs. Load van. Drive home. Lead dog rests head in lap. Re-examine lifelong nonviolent attitudes and beliefs. Kennel dogs. Hobble into house. Husband struggles gallantly to maintain straight face. Mumbles something about the *sole* of a musher. Soak foot.

Other trips went so completely effortlessly—and Max behaved so perfectly—that I could not fathom the reasons for the terrible behaviour. He had had episodes of this totally criminal behaviour since he was a tiny pup. We left him with my parents one time when he was about six months old while we were off on a trip. Because they had a farm (read: prey—cats, chickens, and cows), he was to be tied when outside. We had moved his big wooden doghouse to the farm with him. The first day, he was tied out for a few minutes, rope fastened tightly to the heavy doghouse. My father happened to look out the window to see the doghouse moving rapidly down the road away from the farm. When we returned, we found Max tied to the doghouse and the doghouse tied to a large tree. There were no more offers to babysit their grand-dog.

Max was diabolical in his ability to find a weak spot and take advantage of it. Although our house (with him in it) was nothing if not neat, one night he destroyed a book that Larry was reading, *The Saviour*. This happened while Larry was making a snack. When I came home, Larry said angrily, "Max ate *The Saviour*!" Learned helplessness had taken over, and I was only able to respond, "Oh. And I wasn't even expecting Him tonight!"

Even our young nieces and nephews weren't safe from his tricks. He loved them and enjoyed playing outside with them. His play dates were short-lived, though, because he would purposely slam them with his shoulder, knocking them down each time they started running. He often stole vegetables from the garden—tomatoes, cucumbers, and beets. Although he had not been allowed in the formal living room since he was a pup—and knew that very well— he would suddenly dart into the middle of the room and back out so quickly that he was out of the living room before we could even get our mouths open to berate him.

Max was a challenge and a devil, but one of my favourite memories is of him, at 13 years of age, standing on the kitchen table and eating the butter.

Chapter 3—The Cost of Calls

There are very real costs to providing veterinary care. Each practitioner must buy, rent, or lease each and every piece of equipment in his or her hospital. Plus, each practitioner must maintain supplies of drugs, prescription dog and cat food, surgical instruments, catheters, IV equipment, anaesthetic machines, blood analysers, X-ray units, and so on. All those things enable vets to treat most immediate emergencies and general medical and surgical needs. Unlike medical doctors, veterinarians must stock most of the drugs used in animal medicine in the event that they are needed. We use drugstores a lot less than our counterparts in the Medicare system. To illustrate this point, I remember asking a pharmacist for a common medication and being met with total silence when I asked if it came in tuna flavour. Unfortunately, my cats strongly resent cherry-flavoured medications.

Rather than assuming the best of care for every patient—for example, sending every bad fracture to an orthopaedic specialist—veterinarians realize that some owners are unwilling or unable to pay for a specialist's services. Thus, we are sometimes forced to try less ideal treatments to try to manage the condition. It can be very hard when a lovely young dog is brought in with injuries that require a specialist's management, but referral is not an option. Though some conditions can be treated with less than ideal management (and can result in an acceptable outcome), others require appropriate intervention to obtain a reasonable quality of life. When it boils down to dollars and cents in these cases, it can be extremely hard to look at these patients with the knowledge that they could be saved if funds were available. Also, practical owners may not see the sense in sending very old dogs for expensive intervention. It is a problem that veterinarians struggle with constantly. I understand the situation completely, but my job is not to make financial decisions for my clients. Rather, I aim to guide them into an acceptable resolution of the problem. The acceptable answer to one person's problem may not satisfy the next person in a similar set of circumstances. I try very hard not to take control of the pet from the owner's hands. So often, I hear owners explain their reluctance to bring an animal in for treatment by saying, "I thought you would make me put her down." Because my job is to advocate for the animal, my patient, I may try to make the owner see that the animal is suffering despite my treatment. I may inform the owner of an unwelcome option. At other times, my job is to explain the probabilities of a treatment working in the context of the pet's situation.

One such case was that of a 16-year-old spaniel with a very loud heart murmur who had been hit by a car. Her owner declined a referral to the Veterinary Teaching Hospital at the Atlantic Veterinary College in P.E.I. Instead, he said, "Just fix her up, doc." (He really said that—he called me *doc!*) Despite my stated fears that her broken bone would not heal without a plate to stabilize the fracture—and that her heart murmur made anaesthesia very risky and was best done with specialists in attendance—he replied, "No, you do it, doc." I reiterated the risks involved, and my very real fear that she might pass away under anaesthesia. Still, he asked me to try. With great care, I put the old dog under anaesthesia, reduced her fracture, and stabilized it with a splint. She recovered from the anaesthetic well, and she was discharged to her owner with dire warnings that the splint may not hold the bone securely—and even if it did, her advanced age might mean that the bones would not heal. He was to keep her strictly confined and allow no running, jumping, or exercise at all—to do so was to severely jeopardize the dog's chances of recovery. Two weeks later, I saw this dog to replace her splint, which she had broken trying to walk on it. The bones were still in good alignment, and again, I strongly advised the owner to keep her confined to allow healing. The next week (and the one after that), I replaced her broken splints. Afraid that her activity would cause movement at the fracture site and prevent healing, I lectured the owner at every opportunity, but to no avail. Finally, I was forced to remove splint number six because it too was broken, and the owner was anxious to leave it off (the dog was keeping him awake *clomp-clomping* around his bedroom at night). X-rays revealed that the bone had a good callus over the fracture site (it looked healed), and I removed the splint for the last time. I cautioned him to keep her quiet and to very gradually increase her activity. Then I watched, open-mouthed, as the dog bolted from the clinic, leaped down the five stairs to the ground, bounced to his truck, and leaped onto the seat beside him. I believe I may have said a quiet prayer that she would not break the leg again until I was off call, but I can't be sure that is accurate. Despite the activities that this old dog engaged in—and despite her age—she healed well and regained her ability to be active (not that she had slowed much anyway).

These situations are ones that I love. That dog shouldn't have healed properly. And even if it had, the odds were great that the leg would have been crooked, causing problems following cast removal (given the amount of rough use the leg received). The fact that she healed so well is more a testament to nature than to nurture. Still, I did not correct clients who commented on the great job that I had done on that dog. I simply responded, "Yes, she's a great old girl, isn't she?"

There have been several memorable times when I have enjoyed being wrong—and some when I really dreaded being wrong. As a new veterinarian on call for emergencies (in spite of my lack of experience), I was expected to cope with the same types of cases that my more experienced mentors had. That might mean that I called a friend for advice, called an experienced vet, or used the collection of books that were available to guide veterinarians through those first-time-ever cases. Now, seventeen years later, I am still wrestling with firsts—the first time I have seen a particular type of tumour, the first time I have seen a particular condition, that sort of thing. I suspect that there are still many firsts to come, but they are not nearly as nerve-racking as those initial firsts.

In one case, it seemed that every veterinarian that I knew had left the area for the long weekend when a new client called with the news that he had run over his own cat as it was lying in the driveway. He thought that he had run over her abdomen, and he said that she seemed to be having difficulty breathing. My heart rate was bounding at the thought of the potential injuries, and I gave him directions to my clinic. I tried to quickly read the salient points of each possible injury. The list was long: ruptured bladder, fractured pelvis, collapsed lungs, broken ribs, back injuries, tears in the body wall resulting in hernias, haemorrhage, damaged intestines, and a lacerated liver, to name only a few! These were just some of the potential results of the accident, and multiple combinations of them were highly likely if his assessment was correct. At least I had a list of conditions to rule out when the cat arrived. I was as ready as I could be.

The cat's arrival was anticlimactic in my mind. She was alert and breathing relatively normally. She had a slightly rapid respiratory rate, her colour was good, her limbs seemed intact, her lungs sounded normal ... except for that gurgling sound. What would be gurgling in the chest of a cat that looked this stable? Or even in an unstable cat? Then it hit me! Again my heart rate accelerated. I'd seen this once before as a second-year summer student at the veterinary college where I had worked in the small animal surgery. I knew that I faced one of those "new vet" nightmare scenarios. In my heart of hearts, I knew: the car's weight had forced the cats intestines through the muscular barrier that separates the chest from the abdomen. The diaphragm muscle had been torn, and the cat now had some of her intestines sitting in her chest (alongside her heart and lungs). Hoping for the best, I listened again. Nope, the gurgle was still there. The gurgle, I knew, was the sound of the intestines getting on with their job of digesting her food. I also knew that the damage would need to be repaired as soon as possible.

With my professional face firmly in place, I brought the news to the cat's owner. I gave him my best recommendation: the cat should be taken to the Veterinary Teaching Hospital in Prince Edward Island for surgical repair of the diaphragmatic tear and for observation and treatment of the potential complications of this injury. My reasons were sound. The injuries were severe and not limited only to the diaphragm. The cat's bladder was also outside the body wall, and the abdominal muscles were no longer attached to the pelvis, thus allowing the remaining abdominal organs to settle outside the muscle and under the skin of the belly. Repair of the diaphragm would require at least two veterinarians, and ideally, they would be assisted by multiple support staff. During the procedure that was needed, one vet would have to breathe for the cat while the hole was being repaired. An operating room assistant would be required, and the cat would need intensive care monitoring and nursing care for several days post-surgery. I was a single veterinarian with a single staff member.

The owner, though concerned for his cat, refused my offer of referral adamantly. He asked me to do what I could to save her. After explaining how the odds of her survival plummeted drastically in my inexperienced hands, I told him that, with no ICU available, no anaesthesiologist, no specially trained surgeon to do the surgery, and no one available to monitor her round the clock (I would be on call for three more days), her chances were slim. I attempted to sway his decision in favour of the cat's survival. Finally, however, I accepted his immovable stand on transferring her for experienced and appropriate care. I was reluctant to give up and recommend euthanasia, so I began to make my plans. Fortunately, a neighbouring colleague, Rob, was free at that moment, and he agreed to do the anaesthesia for me. While awaiting his arrival, I repeatedly cautioned the owner that his cat would not likely survive the operation. I had him sign surgical consents that reflected my pessimism.

My reasoning went something like this: if I do not attempt the surgery, the cat will have to be euthanized because her injuries are not compatible with long-term survival. I will make sure that the owner has been well-informed of the dangers of the situation, and that he is aware that my clinic is a poor arena in which to attempt this battle. I will assure myself that he is well aware that there are far greater warriors than I, more seasoned warriors capable of putting forth an effort far more likely to be successful. If I am assured that he has no intention of availing himself of those opportunities, I must attempt to return her to her life as a housecat—certainly not unscathed, but relatively functional. A plan of attack was formed and reviewed with my colleague, and our battle began.

With fierce concentration, I set about opening the abdomen, pulling her intestines back down into their intended position, and carefully closing the ragged tear in her diaphragm while Rob forced oxygenated air into her lungs at a steady rate. Then I returned her remaining organs to her abdominal cavity where they belonged, and I did my best to reattach her muscles to her pelvis. This was quite a feat for such a neophyte, but we both persevered until the cat was finally rebuilt and her abdomen closed.

Although long, the surgery was successful —much to the surprise of both veterinarians involved. The owner left for the night, having been informed that, although the surgery went well, his cat was unlikely to awaken from the anaesthetic. The next morning, he was informed that she had recovered well from the anaesthetic, but she was unlikely to make it through the day. That evening, I was forced to report to him that she had done well throughout the day, and she had started eating on her own, but the next two days would really tell the tale. Having survived the first seventy-two hours, my feeling was that she would likely succumb to some delayed effects of contusions to her heart and lungs. Finally, I was forced to discharge the cat to her owners, but I gave them strict instructions that she was not to run, jump, or exercise strenuously. To allow her to do so was to put stress on the sutures holding her abdominal muscles in place, which would cause them to tear free. Three weeks later, I held a purring, well-healed, happily breathing cat in my arms at her final recheck visit. Even with this tangible, irrefutable evidence of healing and health purring loudly in my arms, I was unable to accept that she had recovered so well. Her owner laughed when I admonished him to keep her quiet and keep her inside.

Both Rob and I were amazed at the success of the surgery and her quick recovery. There is a saying that veterinarians use when discussing the ability that cats have to heal their fractured bones. They say that if you put a cat and its broken bone in the same room, it will heal. (Don't try this at home—it's just a saying!) This situation convinced me that cats, especially this one, have an amazing ability to heal much more than their bones—as long as they are in the same room.

Chapter 4—Freeman and Me

"Can I ask a really big favour?" The phone call was from my colleague, and I thought her voice had a tinge of desperation to it.

"Sure," I replied. Shannon was an associate at a neighbouring practice who had been a good friend and a great help to me when I needed it. "What can I help with?" I asked.

"Well," she started, "I got a call from a woman the other night about a stray dog that they had seen. People were shooting at it, trying to kill it." (Like me, she was constantly trying to save the innocent animals in the area whose owners and neighbours felt that, as animals, their lives were worthless.)

"She said it was a nice lab-cross pup, about 40 pounds. Although she had been feeding it, she couldn't keep it. She wanted it removed before someone killed it. I went to pick it up, and it turned out to be a large German shepherd cross with absolutely no training." (Here, her voice took on a higher pitch and a more urgent tone.) "I brought him with me. I'm staying with my parents this week, so I've had him four days. And I have not slept since he came. He has paced and peed on the floor nonstop the whole time. He is walking around my room all night, leaving S-shaped trails of urine everywhere he goes. I've done everything I know how to do, and I have not gotten him to lie down for more than two minutes."

There were tears in her voice, along with the desperation. "Last night was so bad that I got up in the night, slopped across the urine-soaked floor, and drove all the way across town to the clinic. I got a sedative for him and some Valium for me!" (She began sniffing.) "After two doses of a sedative, he slept for ten minutes. I didn't sleep at all. My parents are mad, I'm exhausted, the whole house is in an uproar and smells like urine!" (She sighed.) "Could you just take him for a couple of days, just until I get a little sleep?"

"Bring him down," I said. We'd had many, many dogs over the years, and I had attended and taught many obedience classes. I felt confident in my abilities and the dog containment setup at our home.

An hour later, Shannon's brother arrived at the clinic, straining to control the large black and tan shepherd-type dog that was seeking to explore the entire clinic in the first ten seconds.

"Here's the beast," he said as he made his escape. "His name is Freeman." Freeman immediately jumped onto the waiting room chairs, knocking books from the tables and creating the biggest uproar that my staff had ever seen.

How bad could he be? I thought, as I darted around the clinic trying to catch the excited dog. He had a way of ducking just before your fingers closed over his collar—and of mouthing your outstretched hand, apparently in an attempt to avoid being caught. *Poor guy,*

I thought, *He's obviously not had any training or attention, and he doesn't know how he should act. No problem, I've rehabilitated several of these dogs. He'll learn a lot from just watching my dogs.*

"Freeman, *stay!*" I ordered. I was beginning to raise my voice. He had eaten three bowls of cat food in his flying trips around the building. He was spilling water bowls and scattering Frank and Richard, the clinic cats, like so much irate fluff. Urine leaked from his penis and left trails behind him. Mentally, I booked him for a urinalysis and some blood work, but we'd have to catch him first! I was thankful that he had arrived at lunchtime—we had no audience to our ineffectual attempts to corral him. Finally, he was caught and leashed. He admitted defeat temporarily while we fussed over him, attempting to settle him and elicit some acceptable behaviour. In our presence, he would not settle. He constantly mouthed our hands, arms, and ankles with enough abandon to leave tooth-shaped bruises on our abused appendages. My assistant, Janice, wished me luck that night as Freeman dragged me from the clinic. She'd voiced the same wish to me as I left with previous rescued dogs, but I sensed a whole different meaning in her words this time.

Our home had been a temporary home to countless abandoned, stray, or rescued dogs, and our eight permanent residents—themselves rescued—had become accustomed to the sudden appearance of another in their midst. Their normal reaction was to thoroughly sniff the newcomer, assert their position in the pack, and then invite a game. I left the details to the dogs as long as no blood was shed. I did not interfere in their group dynamics because I was certain that they understood the dynamics much better than I ever could. After a brief introduction outside, I let Freeman loose in the house with the intent of letting the alpha dog in first, and then gradually letting in the rest. Freeman flew around the house, barking out the windows at our dogs and leaking urine in S-shaped puddles during his travels.

"Let's just crate him for now," suggested Larry, who had yet to fully place his hands on the dog. After a quick game of duck and weave, I was finally able to catch hold of his collar and guide him into the crate. To our surprise and delight, he fell asleep immediately and slept soundly all night.

"Well," Larry explained while we scrubbed up the floors, "he was so tired from keeping Shannon awake for four days, he needed the rest!"

That was the beginning of a frustrating and unsuccessful attempt to rehabilitate Freeman to the point that a new owner could adopt him. After the loss of several pairs of expensive sandals (he only ate the leather upper part), we determined that our closet doors had to be closed completely—even a small crack could be used to open them. I realized this one morning while showering. I felt a cool draft and looked down to see his soaked face, eyes squinting and blinking against the shower spray. He was looking up at me as if to say "Whatcha doin'". Trials proved that he could open the sliding shower door if he had just a one-quarter inch opening.

Attempts at leash training were somewhat successful—after the obligatory duck and weave to get his leash on. He learned to walk at heel relatively quickly and eagerly, but suddenly, out of nowhere, he would start to mouth at arms and legs and jump up in play attempts. It took several minutes to get this behaviour under control. This unpredictability and disrespect made walks with him less than relaxing.

Attempts to integrate him into the pack failed as well. Our dogs tolerated him and initially tried to play, but their yelps of pain and refusal to have any more to do with him told us that he did not know bite inhibition (don't bite too hard when playing). He ran with our group of dogs, constantly barking and annoying them, but he was never part of the group. His constant harassment of one dog, Mick, often resulted in attacks by Mick, which were backed up by the other dogs. Mick, a calm collie mix, would ignore Freeman's constant barking at him until he could stand it no longer. His attack was a signal for the others to release their pent-up frustration with Freeman, and they would all chase him to the far side of their two-acre run. Freeman always looked surprised and amazed at this treatment, but he soon returned to harassing Mick. The pack routinely ousted him from their area next to the house and chased him as far away as possible. Sadly, we crossed out "plays well with others" from his personality profile.

It was shortly after he came—when I was spending as much time as possible attempting to coerce some civilized behaviour from him—that I realized he had become bonded to me. I would find my belongings in his crate, and I soon realized that he could open the laundry hamper. That realization hit when, upon walking into my bedroom, I noted Freeman on my bed, lying on a pair of my blue jeans and a sweatshirt that I had worn recently. One ear was flipped inside out, and my bra was neatly placed on his head. One cup was draped over his other ear, and the strap crossed his forehead above his eye and protruded from the opposite side of his mouth. He liked nothing more than to get into our bedroom. Countless times, I caught him sneaking in there. On one occasion, when I did not catch him, I opened the bedroom door to find my bed totally stripped. Shredded sheets were strewn around the bed, the bedspread was on the floor along with several pillows—and everything was lightly coated with a fresh layer of still-falling feathers from my favourite pillow. Irrefutable proof of his guilt hung from his jaws, and his brown eyes sparkled with glee as he shook his prize with all his might.

During his first six months with us, the toll rose rapidly. Helplessly, we shrugged and said, "It needed pruning anyway" when he chewed one side (about a quarter) off of our lilac bush. It was as far as he could reach while tied outside for a brief moment to do his business. On another "business" trip, he chewed the block heater cord from our car. No, it wasn't plugged in, and I confess to some ambivalence regarding that. On another trip, he decapitated an innocent decorative snowman, and then he made short work of its hat and scarf—finishing his business on the remains.

Our losses were high with Freeman in our house, and tempers began to fray. Our other dogs and the other rescues had settled in so quickly—and with such little trouble—that we were worried about our ability to help Freeman. When yet another pair of his leather shoes succumbed to Freeman's leather fetish, Larry angrily pointed it out to me. In an attempt to placate him, I reasoned, "Do you know how old that pair of shoes was?" He had worn them at our wedding twenty-eight years earlier. "Well," he asserted, "they were still good!"

With Freeman in our house, we were nothing if not neat. Everything had a place, and doors were carefully closed. This practice came none too early as we were almost barefoot. My favourite pair of black leather dress boots had been the latest victim, and Larry had noticed that Freeman had some well-deserved intestinal upset resulting from that. The next day, our housekeeper had decided to wash Freeman's bed. On noticing some diarrhoea in the crate with black areas in it, she called out to Larry that Freeman had had black diarrhoea. After a short pause, he asked, "Is it as black as your boot?" "Yes," she replied. "It's Mil's boot," he answered.

With a lot of work, Freeman had become manageable in our home. This was aided by our rather high-end dog containment systems: runs in the basement and a two-acre field fenced for dogs. And it didn't hurt that we had a tolerance for all things dog (even abnormal things). I theorized that "Freeby" had been removed from his mother and littermates at a very young age, which is a very poor practice, and then not given the care, attention, and social experiences that would allow him to understand and respond appropriately to canine and human behaviours. We recommend that puppies be left with their littermates and under the influence of their mother until they are seven to eight weeks of age. It is during that period that they teach each other bite inhibition and other dog manners necessary to allow the dog to accept and understand the intentions of a strange dog when they are older. Puppies removed early from their littermates and mother often do not know how to read the body language and gestures of another dog—or how to relate normally to them.

Still, we couldn't give up on Freeman. Didn't he have the right to live, the same as the other strays? Wasn't he good for five or ten minutes in the morning when you could cuddle and stroke him before he started to act up? When he was good, wasn't he very good? Wasn't he markedly improved from our first meeting? We both agreed. Unless a miracle happened and an accepting, experienced dog person offered to take him as a pet, he would stay with us. He would be free in the field, free in the house when we could watch him, and crated at night in our room. We would attempt to make his life as interesting and normal as our other dogs' lives, and we would continue to try to modify his behaviour into some semblance of acceptability.

And so it goes. When the dog's blue, plastic wading pool was emptied, and I was about to refill it for their comfort on one hot day, I saw it moving rapidly, upside down around the field. Closer inspection revealed a black and tan muzzle protruding from a six-inch hole at the base of the pool. He had chewed a hole in the pool, and he was now having a great time with it, racing around the field with it flapping behind him like some great, round blue plastic cape. Cape or not, Superdog, he wasn't!

Still, we persevered. We felt that love and patience—along with firm, consistent rules—would eventually improve his behaviour. I left with colleagues to attend a conference in Halifax, Nova Scotia, one weekend. As I was packing, Freeman was in the bedroom with me, under my close scrutiny. It wasn't until I was dressing for bed the first night away that I became aware of his diabolical and sneaky behaviour. He had chewed a large hole in the side of my nightie. My roommates, aware of my troubles with this dog, roared with laughter.

There was good reason he became known as "The Schemin', Screamin', Demon Freeman." Given that his un-doglike behaviour in our pack made him an outcast, he always had to be kennelled separately from the others for his own safety. And if he were released while the others were kennelled, he would run around their fences barking and hurtling insults until the others finally responded by doing the same. In frustration, Larry commented, "That Freeman is the epicentre of all our pack problems!" In his run, he would jump straight in the air at his gate, barking continuously while the others played in the field. This was a new one for me. I had observed many tiny poodles jump straight in the air to be picked up by their owners, but the sight of the 80-pound Freak's head repeatedly appearing a foot above his six-foot fence made us both shake our heads in bewilderment and walk away.

The constant barking became a concern as well. Because we had so many dogs coming and going at our residence, we did not want to annoy the neighbours. The SPCA had recommended a device called an Aboistop collar to handle this sort of problem. This was a battery-operated collar filled with citronella oil, which was set off by a loud bark. When triggered, it would spray the oil into the face of the dog. It seemed like the perfect solution. Placed on Freeman, though, it lasted a very short time. Both the battery and the citronella container ran out within the first few hours, leaving us with a very strong smelling (but continually barking) dog. Still, the lemony smell was pleasant, and I suspect that he was not bothered by mosquitoes that summer.

It was with a great feeling of accomplishment, then, when I finally got Freeman trained to lie at my feet while I ate my meals at the coffee table in the living room. Imagine my surprise when I looked down to see him lying on his back, head between my feet, and mouth wide open. I suspect he adopted this position to receive any spillage from my plate. Still, he was not a restful dog. While he was loose in the house with us, we could not relax. "No, Freeman! Get out of the garbage!" (He had opened the door himself.) "No, Freeman! Get off the cupboard!" (He could reach to the very back of the cupboard while standing on his hind feet.) "No, Freeman! Don't tear up that dog bed! No, Freeman! Get out of the closet! No, Freeman! Don't chew that shoe! No, Freeman! Put that roast down! No, Freeman! Get off the sofa! No, Freeman! Don't bite my hands!" He would not be distracted by toys unless he could destroy them. He would not sit and allow us to pat him, not without grabbing and mouthing our hands. And if we did not grab a folded newspaper in self-defence, the encounter would escalate—without movement on our part—to climbing on us and mouthing and biting at any undefended border.

Freeman and I had a two-month period of truce with a marked decrease in his annoying mouthing and jumping behaviour. I had broken my ankle, and I was forced to spend two months hopping about on crutches. If there was a bright side, it was that, if Freeman's behaviour escalated to the point that it was damaging to me, I was able to stop it immediately with one poke of my crutch, deftly aimed at his chest or departing rear. Each poke was preceded by a sharp no!—not that a sharp no had not been tried time and time again with no results. I suspect that the effectiveness of "the big stick" was due to its impressive size and length—and the fact that I could get him with the padded end (even though he used his usual duck and weave to avoid reprisals following his poor behaviour). Whatever the cause and effect, Freeman and I spent a somewhat relaxing two months during which he would lie by my chair and allow me to pat him and rub his chest without resulting bruises. The use of the crutch became unnecessary, as long as it was propped beside my chair in full view. His behaviour with me, though not stellar, was acceptable, and I wondered what would happen when my ankle was again safe to walk on.

Long story short, he reverted to the old Freeman the day I returned the crutches. It was not a total loss, though. I think a slight residue of the enjoyment that he felt at having his chest scratched remains: occasionally, he comes to me and seems to want that done. Although I often comply, after just a few minutes, he begins to mouth at my hands and arms, and he tries to jump in my lap. In sum, I was grateful for the hiatus, but I was nonetheless disappointed. Freeman was back!

Just the other day, as I rested on the sofa, I noted Freeman sneaking past me with a red ball in his mouth. *Wait a minute!* I thought, *The dogs don't have any red balls!* I leapt to my feet to recover the tomato that I too had designs on (it was BLT night). As I tried to catch him, trap him in a corner, and intimidate him into dropping it, I wondered what I would do with it if I did successfully retrieve my tomato. Finally, trapped between the wood stove and the chair, the tension of the chase got to him. Eyes wide, backed against the wall, he regarded me tensely. Suddenly, seeds and juice squirted from his mouth, staining my jeans. The remainder disappeared down his gullet with two chomps of his huge jaws—another win for the demon dog.

Freeman's poor manners extended to guests as well. Although his intentions were good—he was happy to greet people—his mode of greeting was less than princely. As one friend commented recently (having just been greeted very familiarly by Freeman): "Well, I guess I just got my Christmas goose!"

Although we try very hard to treat Freeman in the same way that the others are treated—and allow him to enjoy the same perks that the others enjoy—he is very trying. Just recently, it was his turn to accompany me on my hour-long walk. We enjoyed what I felt was an hour of mutual camaraderie with interesting and appealing terrain, intermittent flavourful treats, and the release of pent-up energies in a companionable, uplifting circumstance. He had been a delight, as he is sometimes when on lead. We had even survived an attempted attack by a leashed German shepherd. Freeman reacted very well— and without stepping out of the heel position. His only response had been a disdainful glare at his attacker that clearly said, "Oh, grow up!" Why, then, on our return home and in our own yard, would he sit perfectly on my left in the heel position only until his leash was removed? Why would he cross in front of me and disappear behind me, back down the driveway and away? A thorough search of our community found Freeby chest-deep in the swampy field just outside the village sewage treatment facility. A small stream runs there, and I would like to believe that the stream alone is responsible for the wet terrain and black, foul-smelling mud that caked his legs and chest. Still, its proximity to the treatment facility gives me doubts. I feel that my act of encouraging the mud-coated Freeman into my rather new car will stand me in good stead at the pearly gates. I also feel that my unwavering voice offering him a lovely cookie if he would only defile my car with suspect mud and bad behaviour would win an Academy award for me—if only someone other than the dog had heard it! There was no trace in my voice of my actual feelings toward Freeman at that point; otherwise, he would not have graced my car with his disgusting and smelly presence. Damn him!

Despite Freeman's shortcomings—and he had many—Larry decided that he would remain with us permanently. His reasoning? Freeby gets a little better every year. If that dog lives to be 20, he may come close to displaying acceptable behaviour. And I know what he'll do next: he'll spitefully die of old age, just days after reaching that coveted state.

In the meantime, as we struggle to coexist, our feelings range from sympathetic and protective to exasperated and helpless. He still has the ability to upset the rest of the pack (and us) by fence fighting, stealing toys, and destroying whatever he can reach. As Larry said long ago, "Freeman really is the epicentre of the problems with our pack!"

Chapter 5—Don't Fence Me In

N ot long after our last malamute passed away, a man brought a tiny grey pup to the clinic. He said he had found her in the woods a long distance from any homes. He could not leave her there to die, and the local shelters were unable to accept her, so he decided to find help for her. He offered to pay the initial emergency fees if I would accept and treat the pup. He'd heard that I helped strays.

In his arms was a limp Siberian husky pup with the most amazing blue eyes. She could barely open them. She had severe bloody diarrhoea and vomiting, and she was dangerously dehydrated. With her young life teetering on the edge, I couldn't refuse to try to help. At first glance, I was almost certain that she had a disease called parvovirus, which is common in unvaccinated dogs.

Parvovirus attacks the lining of the intestinal tract—the stomach and intestines—and untreated, it often causes severe dehydration and a painful death with severe stomach and abdominal cramping spasms. Puppy vaccinations, starting at seven to eight weeks of age, would have easily prevented this and spared the pup the devastating and painful effects of the disease. With intense nursing care, intravenous fluids, and antibiotics, however, there was a chance that the pup might recover. The pup moaned and made a weak attempt at raising her head. I told the man that I would try to save her, but I couldn't guarantee anything. He did not want her back. With two weeks of intensive care nursing, the severely ill pup survived the disease and eventually moved to our house until a permanent home could be found.

Larry, a *Star Trek: Voyager* fan, named her Seven (of Eight) after his favourite character in the show: the gorgeous Seven of Nine. Seven, typical of the Arctic breeds, was very intelligent, extremely loving, beautiful to look at, and very difficult to keep at home. Our home was on a hill overlooking an elementary school, and Seven, who loved children, would often sit on the lawn with her tail wagging, watching them play.

Larry had fenced off a two-acre area of our property to allow the dogs to play and do dog things because we were busy—we did not have time to give them sufficient daily exercise to make them "good and tired." (Or do I mean "tired and good"?) Walking eight big dogs would be a full-time job for someone. We could exercise all eight dogs with a rousing game of fetch, but we were always desperately trying to keep five balls flying at once.

Larry had carefully blocked any perceived escape routes in or under the fencing, and our dogs (and the many strays who had passed through our hands) had respected the boundaries. Seven, too, was fine—initially. When she was about a year old, Larry took her to the school to talk about dog bite prevention. Seven had a great time—children everywhere, and all the attention was centred on her! She met and loved the teachers as well. A few days after her visit, we got a call from the principal of the school. The paramedics were there to demonstrate their job and equipment, but they couldn't work because Seven was in their vehicle, lying on the stretcher. Could we pick her up at the principal's office?

Horrified, we raced to the school to retrieve our dog. She hung her head out of the opened window of our car as if waving to her fans as we drove away. Larry searched for an opening in the fence where she might have escaped and found a small hole, freshly dug, on the far side of the enclosure. That was quickly fixed with large boulders to discourage digging in those types of areas.

Several weeks later, we received another call from the school. Seven had arrived and visited all the classes in turn. The children, who all knew her name by now, were delighted, but we were asked to pick her up because the teachers couldn't get their classes to focus. This time, she had climbed the fence using a tree as a boost and run to visit her friends.

As Larry left the school, Seven, seeing a group of children in the gym, slipped her collar and ran directly to them. Delight was emanating from her face. Larry, forced to interrupt the session, followed her into the gym—no delight was apparent on his face at all. He then added four feet to the height of the fence near the large trees on one side of the enclosure.

A week later, the patient principal called again for us to pick up our student. As we left embarrassed, the teachers called out to Seven, reminding her not to forget her homework. Larry found a small opening between the added wire and a tree where she had escaped.

This all required planning and persistence, and we feared that she would be hit by a car eventually. We were also concerned about the poor example we were setting (after all, our dog was running free). After another escape, we were desperate. We hadn't been worried about the other dogs getting out, but we were afraid that they might follow her lead. Thus, we turned to a trainer who recommended that we try a shock collar whenever she tried to escape. I was strongly resistant to training dogs with this method.

Our only other option had been to tie the dog because she had been escaping even as we called to her to stop. We had been forced to tie her to a 100-foot rope in the enclosure. This was far from the life we wanted for her, so we invested in an underground fence. Those fences were highly recommended, and I had seen how effective they could be. We got the fence package and about three kilometres of wire. We spent an entire weekend installing it, and then we spent the majority of the next few weeks training her in that system.

"There!" we said as we walked to greet some friends who had arrived in our yard. "At least she'll stay in the pen now." We then gazed in disbelief as she sailed past us to greet our visitors. "She climbed right over the fence," they laughed as they ruffled her fur and praised her beauty and intelligence. We would have preferred a stupid dog at that point!

"Maybe it isn't working," I suggested. But we had all heard the warning beep as Seven approached the fence. If the dog does not stop at the warning beep, it receives a shock that encourages it to stop and move away from the fence.

"I'll check," Larry said. He took Seven's collar off and approached the fence himself. Despite the warning beep, he continued to approach until, suddenly, he let out a yelp, flung the offending collar away from himself, and grabbed his hand. "Jeez!" he exclaimed. "That has quite a wallop!" Placing the collar back on Seven, he watched her wander around, often stimulating the beep mechanism by approaching the fence. But she responded only with a quick scratch at her neck where the collar touched. Could she be scratching at a fly?

"Let's try it on another dog," he suggested, and he brought our foxhound mix from his run. Placing the collar on Dusty, he released him and watched in horror as the hound raced to the fence and then dropped, howling with fear and surprise. Scooping Dusty up in his arms, he removed him from the field of the collar, crooning, "I'm sorry! I'm sorry, Dusty. It's okay! I'm sorry!"

"Maybe the collar is not touching her properly," I conjectured, and I clipped the thick double coat from the area where the prongs were meant to touch. Again, we released her and watched with amazement as beep after beep sounded while she explored the fence line. She paused now and then to scratch at her collar. Was it flies? Did she feel it at all?

Frustration had set in. What could we do to allow this active dog to play with the others (without annoying the neighbours) and still be safe from traffic? During one escape, she chased the neighbour's cat, which had been sunning itself outside on its rope. Both ran into the house and to the upstairs bedroom. Although not interested in attacking cats, she loved to chase them if they ran from her. As the local vet, I felt that the situation was unacceptable (to have my dog chasing my patients). Despite our attempts to keep her exercised on a leash, Seven became destructive, chewing at the beds in the runs where we were forced to keep her. She could see the other dogs playing and running in the fenced field. Those dogs never went near the fence, not even when there were people nearby. We reasoned that, if we electrified the fence so it gave her a jolt if she touched it, wouldn't that teach her to stay away from it? And wouldn't that solve our problem while letting her romp at will with the other dogs?

The next several days (and many dollars) were spent setting up the system. It was much like the electrified fences used by farmers to keep their cattle in. A strand of the wire is connected to a battery, and the fence gives a shock if touched. Patiently, Larry removed the old underground fencing that he had previously installed, and then he added extra (and expensive) metal posts and insulators. As we set up this system, we both voiced our misgivings, but we reasoned that Seven was the only one who ever got that close to the fence. Therefore, she would be the only one being reprimanded.

Seven was released alone into the field, and we quickly heard a yelp as she tried to make her escape. Guiltily, we noted that she had jumped back from the fence and looked very frightened.

"Well," Larry commented in our defence, "maybe now we can keep her in and save her from being hit and killed by a car." Several shocks later, we felt that Seven had truly given up on escaping. We let the other dogs out with her to play in the field. To our knowledge, they never approached the fence physically, and they were in no danger from it. Seven, the leader of the games, started the chase down the hill and into the small wooded area at the far side of the field. Grinning, we watched for some time as the pack played and explored and did dog things. Smiling, we returned to the house for lunch, proud that we had bested our little rival.

Suddenly, we heard a yelp, followed by another and another. Rushing outside, we found seven dogs huddled on the picnic table that we keep in the run for them to lie on. The eighth dog, Seven, was sniffing around the field, no doubt hunting rodents (that was her favourite pastime). No amount of encouragement, apologies, or begging would convince those dogs to get down from the table.

We thought, *Let's bring them in for the day and start again in the morning.* The dogs rushed into the house and clung to our sides all evening. Our sense of self-worth had plummeted in view of the terrible fears we had inflicted on seven of our eight dogs. We thought that things might look better to the dogs in the morning, but that was not so. They stepped through the door into the field only on our orders. And they rushed to the picnic table and huddled together, staring mournfully and pitifully at us.

"That's it!" exclaimed Larry. "I'm not having my dogs upset like that!" Rapidly, he unhooked the battery and disarmed our weapon. As if aware of that fact, the seven dogs slowly disembarked from our picnic table and cautiously began to move around the field. Twenty minutes later, the school called, asking us to come pick up Seven—she was disrupting their school concert. Heads hanging in defeat, we retrieved our Houdini and again brought her home. The following week, Larry spent every free moment adding wire to the fence, filling areas with boulders, nailing logs to the bottom of the fence, and trying to block every imaginable avenue of escape.

A short while ago, I received a call from my neighbour's son, saying that he had found a dog with a tag on the collar. "Is there a name on the tag?" I asked. "Yes," he replied, "it says *Steven.*" I quickly drove over to pick up Seven, who was enjoying her neighbourly visit.

Following an escape on my watch, I drove around the neighbourhood in ever-widening circles. Eventually, I sat in the car in my yard, fear for her life foremost on my mind. Was she lying injured or dead in a ditch somewhere? I had checked and rechecked all her favourite haunts. I knew she was not at my brother's farm because I could see all of his cattle grazing peacefully. She was not at the school. With increasing fear, I decided to take one more drive around in hopes of finding some sign of her. Next, I would begin checking the ditches. Two hundred yards up the main road, almost in front of the school, I met Seven. She was proceeding south in the centre of the northbound lane, head held unnaturally high to avoid dragging and tripping over her prey: a very large and very dead groundhog. Despite my attempts to act casually and hide my relief at seeing her, my horror at the sight of her kill and my anger at her most recent escape were evident. Head hanging, she dropped the poor groundhog and slunk to the car door. Foiled again! Again, Larry and I walked the fences, plugging every imagined escape route. The other dogs had no interest in escaping—they had even watched her leave.

Seven still patrols the fences, looking for the slightest change, the slightest flaw in the fence that she might exploit. If I had had any idea that we had adopted an escape artist all that time ago, I would certainly have named her Rover or Shep. Anything is better than circling the neighbourhood shouting, "Seven!" At least we didn't call her *Four*. And so it goes.

Last month, as Larry entered the school looking for Seven, he was met with the following: "No, Seven isn't here." This was said before he could even ask. Even as I write, he is scouring the neighbourhood in search of her. Though Seven's escapes have become fewer and farther between, it is still a battle of wills. And if one looks closely enough at the weed-covered fence, one can still see the yellow insulators from that terrible electric fence, long unused, but testament to our desperate attempts to keep one little husky safe at home.

Chapter 6—Humour Helps

Veterinary medicine gives us great breadth of experience. Through my studies and my work, I have learned to appreciate both the animals and their owners as special and unique individuals. One of my favourite uncles once said that you have to be 40 to appreciate a tree. Now I know what he meant.

I am very happy to be the owner of a small animal clinic in rural New Brunswick, and I have learned so much on my road to that end. I have learned to appreciate the special people and animals that I have been privileged to meet.

I have very much enjoyed the sense of humour that I see in so many of my clients—and their ability to see the funny side of their situations. One example is the client who brought her dog in to have porcupine quills removed from his face. In describing the incident resulting in the encounter with the porcupine, she said, "He just went around the corner of the garage and came back a few minutes later saying, 'Sumpin' wong wif m' mouf!'"

I also enjoy a chance to demonstrate my own sense of humour. When Jennifer, my sister-in-law, came to the clinic carrying a large white cat, she told me that a miracle had happened and they had finally found their long-lost pet. After a thorough examination, I took great delight in informing her that a second miracle had occurred, and that I would have to neuter him again!

One of my favourite stories is about Janice, my assistant. She had gotten two malamute pups from us, and no dogs ever received better care than those two. Although they always had options (warm kennels, going into the house), Janice worried about them when they were outside during inclement weather instead of in the house. One particular day, she called us for advice and got Larry on the phone.

"Larry," she asked, "what would you do if your dogs had warm, insulated dog houses and were lying outside in the freezing rain?"

"Oh," he replied, "make a sandwich, watch TV." We had become used to the malamutes' enjoyment of the weather, and we allowed them to do as they wished.

During my summers as a vet student, I was very lucky to be hired to work in the small animal clinic operating room as assistant to the operating room nurse. That summer, there was a dog in the clinic, Lucky. He was a small, blond collie mix. He had been badly injured when hit by a car, and he had undergone several painful surgeries. He was unable to walk, and he had little interest in food. His depression had everyone worried, and we tried to give him extra attention whenever possible. I would carry Lucky outside during my lunch break and try to tempt him with special treats placed just out of his reach. He was starting to try to move toward the treats, something that I was very excited about. I wanted him to show interest and attempt to move, and I had invested in many tantalizing goodies to tempt him. One day, the OR nurse came into the OR room where I was assisting with a long procedure. She relieved me so I could go for lunch. Because I wanted her to be able to find me if I was needed, I said, "I'm going to get Lucky." Lifting his head from his work, the surgeon asked, "In a half-hour lunch break?"

Another story that I like pertains to a pup that I obtained from animal control just before she was about to be put down. She was yet another victim of the attitude that prevails that assigns little value to the lives of cats and dogs or the process of spaying and neutering pets to prevent overpopulation. Because this was a common occurrence for animal control—and because they had no facilities to house these "throwaway" animals—we took her in to try to place her. During the period that she lived with me, I simply called her *Puppy*. Shortly before we found a home for her, we decided that she needed a real name. Because she already answered to Puppy, we simply changed it to Poppy. She was a little black pup with a broad head that seemed to look more and more like a pit bull's. Although we do not subscribe to the "pit bulls are evil" belief, we nevertheless screen any of the interested applicants very carefully. We would never want one of our rescues, regardless of breed, to fall into the wrong hands. Although she was too young to make any real breed distinction, I still worried. I voiced my concerns to my brother, John. Laughing, he bent over the tiny puppy and advised, "Use your powers for good!" Poppy took his advice and became a much-loved family member in a family with several children.

A sense of humour is a powerful tool when working with animals, especially multiple animals. The first malamutes that we had—two females that we planned to show in conformation—started our long struggle for peace *and* pets. We felt that it would not be too much to ask. However, before we could get our kennel built, both dogs went into oestrus (commonly known as *heat*), and our yard became very attractive to all the males in the area. Not wanting puppies or messes on our brand new carpets, we built very nice runs in our basement where the dogs spent the night.

It was in late July, and the sun rose very early. It lit up the basement and prompted our dogs to howl to be taken outdoors, their preferred location. Grumbling, we reprimanded them and tried to get them to be quiet until at least 6 a.m. One Saturday morning, when the noise started from our basement shortly after 5 a.m., Larry leapt from the bed and stomped down the basement stairs. Then I heard hammering from several sites down there, and after a time, Larry returned to bed. Aware that he was angry, I chose not to speak and eventually fell asleep again. Several hours later, I awakened to silence and brilliant sunshine. I raced to the basement door, wondering what had happened to the poor dogs. When I opened the door, the basement was in total darkness, and the dogs blinked and squinted their eyes as I turned on the light. Looking around, I saw that he had nailed plywood over every single window! Score one for Larry!

Even the cats that we took in gave us trouble. One, a young orange and white tailless kitten that we had found in a ditch was a challenge. Bob, as we called him, was a sweet, loving, cuddly lap cat during the day, but at night his demon gene manifested. He became the kitten from hell. He would race up and down our sleeping bodies with no respect for faces, eyes, or opened mouths. On one memorable night, I awoke suddenly to Larry sputtering and removing what looked like mud from his mouth. He did not look pleased! Beside my pillow lay the beautiful geranium from the window ledge at the head of our bed. Smugly seated on that ledge was Bob, totally unaware of the danger he had placed himself in.

On another night, we were awakened by the screeching of nails on metal and a pathetic cat cry that seemed to come from under our bed. We had recently been working on the ductwork of our furnace, and we had accidentally left the cover off one of the openings to those ducts just under our bed. Apparently, Bob had gotten in there—via exploration or by accident—and he was now unable to climb out of the curved duct leading up to our room. Since we were then sleeping on a waterbed, there was no thought of moving the bed to allow us to reach down and help him out.

With a long-suffering sigh, Larry got out of bed and trudged to the basement where he separated pieces of the ductwork and tried to reach in to grab Bob. By now, fun had replaced fear, and Bob was having a ball! Larry gently coaxed Bob to the edge of the duct, and as he reached for him, Bob scooted back into the duct just beyond Larry's reach. From my warm nest in the bed, I heard the entire monologue.

"Here, kitty, kitty." (He spoke gently and with warmth.) "Come on, little guy. That's the kitty, just a little farther." (There was a reverberating sound of something hitting aluminum.) "Damn! Come on, little guy. Time to go to bed. Good boy." (There was another *boing* of aluminum under sudden stress.) "Shit! Come on, let's go get some nice kitty food. Come on, Bob. Oh, come o-o-on, Bob!" (Boing!) "I hate cats! Come to papa, Bobby." (He was obviously faking friendliness and warmth.) "That's the boy." (Boing!) "I should leave you in there and make a really big fire!" (And then he began to say in a sweet tone.) "I don't know why we didn't just take you to the dump! That's good, Bobby boy, you have to let me get a little sleep." (There was desperation in his voice now.) "Here, little guy, want some sardines?" (He was speaking through gritted teeth.) (Boing!) "Got you, you little guttersnipe! I should feed you to the dogs! No, you're not getting down, not until I put a book over that duct opening! I hate cats!"

Years later, we rescued an extremely matted, long-haired orange tom that we called Hairy Hairbag. Hairy was a mess. His coat was like a helmet—hard and matted along both his sides. It took hours using Larry's beard trimmers to remove the clumps, and then the sores exposed under the hair required treatment. As I examined Hairy further, I noted a deep, indented scar that ran from the inner corner of his eye to the nostril on the same side. The scar opened at the end and interfered with the flow of air through that side of his nose. Also, one front foot was frozen in the standing position—that is, at a 90-degree angle to his leg. Plus, the long bones of his hind leg had been broken, and the hard point of the displaced but healed bone was easily felt under the skin above his hock. It was more evidence of the injuries sustained by cats who are free-roaming and not neutered. The horror, the pain, the suffering that this cat had endured stunned me. I felt terrible for the suffering that he had so obviously endured with no sign of veterinary attention. I was immediately committed to him, promising that he would never have to endure the likes of that again. As I released him in my house, his reaction after a quick look around seemed to be: "Nice place! Guess I'll stay!" He immediately settled himself in the best seat in the house.

Larry had been away for that weekend, and he returned to find Hairy with his terrible haircut—body bald except for the stripe down the middle of his back, like a Mohawk—walking down our hall. His deformed foot with its long (as yet unclipped) nails was catching in the pile of the rug and forcing him to shake his foot every few steps to free it. His breath wheezed, and he snorted as he moved air in and out of the affected nostril. Still, he gamely continued on to greet Larry. *Thump, snort, wheeze, shake!* And he continued to pull his nails out of the rug. Larry watched him for a few seconds, and then he turned to me saying, "You know, when I pictured us with a cat, I pictured a sleek, graceful creature." The next night, Hairy developed a romantic attachment to Larry's arm in the middle of the night, necessitating a trip to the veterinarian the very next day. Thankfully, my friend and mentor, Dr. Murray Mutrie, easily fixed that problem and left us with some hope that the behaviour would gradually disappear. For his part, Larry was now afraid to close his eyes with Hairy in the room.

Unlike many cats that I have known, Hairy was the undisputed king of the house. He had gone from pathetic ditch cat to king of his world in virtually no time, and his attitude was starting to annoy me. Several times, I remember calling to him to come to me for some cooked chicken. From the kitchen, I could see Hairy in the den, propped against the arm of the sofa. He had a huge belly—the most prominent part of him—and he had huge yellow eyes that met mine and seemed to say, "Bring it over!" I don't even wait on Larry! Through sheer force of personality, he was able to prevent the malamutes from entering the den. As the dogs gathered at the door, Hairy's low but menacing growl caused them to freeze and look at us for help. The only time we could relax in the den with our dogs was after securing Hairy in our bedroom. And then we were forced to listen to his enraged screams. Our prayers were answered one day when my mother asked if Hairy could come and live with her. Other than a small tiff over who was responsible for apprehending a mouse seen in her kitchen, she and Hairy coexisted very well for the rest of his life. (Mom scooped up the mouse and put it outside.)

Another favourite story is about Miles, a young Border collie mix that we rescued. Larry had been away for a few days while Miles was in his adolescent period. During that time, one of Miles's ears had lifted and turned into a twisted, half-erect stance. On his return home, Larry looked at Miles and said, "Miles, you have a new *eardo!*"

Miles and Seven (our husky) became best friends. They played together in the field all day, digging holes in which our lawn tractor often became stuck and dragging branches up from the nearby trees. One afternoon, I came home to Larry's story of finding Miles with his head and shoulders sticking out of a hole recently dug on the side hill near our house. After calling for Miles, he was very surprised to see Seven crawl out of the hole right behind him.

"Wow," I said, "that must have been quite a hole!"

"Seven and a half Miles deep!" he quickly replied.

Chapter 7—Euthanasia:
The "Good" Death

One of the most difficult requests that I face as a veterinarian is the request for what I call *convenience euthanasia.* Frequently, we get requests to euthanize animals because their owners are moving, the dog doesn't like the cat, the dog sheds, the husband doesn't like cats, or—the best one I was told about— "We've moved to a new apartment and the cat doesn't match the rug there." We also get requests to euthanize strays or abandoned animals and those picked up by animal control. Merriam-Webster defines euthanasia as "the act or practice of killing or permitting the death of hopelessly sick or injured individuals (as persons or domestic animals) in a relatively painless way for reasons of mercy."[1] Many people call killing their animals *euthanasia,* but it is just killing. I find this an impossible thing to do. Though I realize that pet overpopulation has left us as a society with little alternative to putting down huge numbers of unwanted cats and dogs, this would be minimized if pets were spayed or neutered. Owners whose pets breed and add to the problem need to take responsibility for

---

1 *Merriam-Webster OnLine*, s.v. "euthanasia," accessed September 9, 2012, http://merriamwebster.com/dictionary/euthanasia.

the deaths of these innocent animals. The success of the "no kill" movement in its recruitment of many shelters in the United States and Canada is promising. I hope that it sweeps both nations and spreads worldwide. At my clinic, we refuse to kill normal, healthy animals. It is a very personal philosophy that makes it impossible for me to participate in the deaths of these lovely dogs and cats, these very sentient beings.

I find it easier to take the animals and look after them until we find homes for them. This is why our house has dogs in every room— and there are many cats in the basement of my clinic. No amount of Febreze will take the kennel smell out of our house, and the windowsills are crisscrossed with the marks of many nails. And talk about yellow snow! As they say, "No good deed goes unpunished"— and we've certainly been punished!

During the latter part of my internship at the Western College of Veterinary Medicine in Saskatoon, Saskatchewan, I became aware of a research/teaching dog who was in danger of being "euthanized." No one had stepped forward to adopt him when his allowed time at the university was up. Impulsively, I took him home. He was a black and tan shepherd mix, and I thought that we would live happily ever after—the dog eternally grateful that I rescued him from death. Chance, as I called him (I was his last chance), knew nothing about home life and stood in the middle of our living room, refusing to move or make eye contact for several hours. It was then that we realized the extent of his lack of socialization. Only the friendship and company of Lacey, our malamute, allowed him to slowly and gradually accept his new life as a house pet.

We immediately started trying to get him used to travelling in the car because we had a long drive from Saskatoon to our home in

Florenceville, New Brunswick, looming in our future. We were at the point where Chance seemed to be able to relax in the van as we made short trips around the city, and we were optimistic that our trip home would go smoothly. Not so!

Although he was securely ensconced in his crate and seated atop his favourite blanket in the rear of the van with his best friend Lacey beside him (along with chews, toys, and food all around him), he started to shriek about 15 minutes outside of Saskatoon. Despite my attempts to sooth and calm him, he was inconsolable. Nothing I could do would help him settle. I put Chance in the crate, got in the crate with him, put him in the crate with Lacey, put him in the front at my feet, put him in my lap, curled up with him on the floor, bribed him with treats, gave him my Gravol (a common medication for motion sickness)—all to no avail. He would stop his shrieking when he was out of the van, but immediately upon returning to the road, he would resume his shrieks at ear-splitting levels. From Saskatoon to Yorkton to Winnipeg to Ontario, past Kenora and Dryden to Thunder Bay, past Wawa and onward to Sault St. Marie, we endured the noise. None of our attempts to settle Chance had the least effect on him.

I was near tears again, just outside of Sault St. Marie. I was sitting in the front seat with my empty Tim Horton's cardboard cup in my hand when I lost it. To my shame, I turned in my seat and bellowed, "*Shut up!*" I hurled the empty cup at Chance who was, at the moment, sitting in front of his crate screaming. Well-known for not being able to hit the broad side of a barn, I lobbed that cup and hit Chance squarely between the eyes. Chance stopped midshriek. He stared at me in (blessed) complete silence. Shocked by what I had done, I too was totally silent. As I turned to Larry, he muttered, "Let's just enjoy this while we can." Unfathomably, for the rest of our drive to New Brunswick, Chance behaved like a normal, quiet dog. He enjoyed his walks when we stopped, chewed his bones and toys to alleviate the boredom of the long drives between stops. He never made a sound. Still appalled by what I had done, I nevertheless wondered whether I had discovered a new behaviour modification technique. Should I write a paper on it? Would I call it the "Tim Horton's Coffee Cup"? Maybe I would call it "The Last Chance Technique." Would I become famous for my discovery, or infamously known as the dog bellower. I couldn't take the chance (if you will). As a new grad, I needed a job—not the reputation this episode would bring me. Like Chance, I just shut my mouth.

In my first job (in Ontario), I was presented with a little white dog found by animal control in a very isolated area outside of the city. The dog was slated for "euthanasia," and the usual reason—overpopulation—was given. I was designated to carry out that action. Looking into the dog's eyes, I knew that I did not want to kill that dog. I rushed out of the exam room and called Larry. In my rush to explain myself—and having not even checked the dog's sex—I babbled, "He's cute, and 'e's little, and 'e's white, and 'e's nice, and 'e's—"

"An *And 'e* dog, is it?" interrupted Larry. I brought that dog home, a female that we called "Andi," of course. She could follow many commands, including rolling over, shaking hands, and speaking when asked. Someone had obviously spent a lot of time with her, and she knew that she was meant to sleep on the bed. I always thought that I would find an ad or see posters about a little white dog that was lost. I never did, and gradually I relaxed and allowed her to be my dog. She looked like a small Samoyed husky with huge ears and eyes that reminded me of Luba Goy, long-time star of the Royal Canadian Air Farce television program. Her demeanour was that of a princess, and she loved to be told how pretty she was. Her character prompted us to label her *Andrea Samoyedski, our little Arctic princess.* She hated to be left in the outdoor pen with the dogs, and she disdainfully growled if one accidentally bumped her. Her place was in the house, lounging on the best seat in the room. Twelve years later, she still has the best seat—even if she has to be helped into it.

Shortly after Andi invaded our lives, I was booked to "euthanize" a large lab-mix stray. The animal control people felt that he would not be adoptable because he had howled constantly while in their custody, and he was decidedly not a favourite. I went to the kennel room where he was held, and I saw a big, goofy, intact black-and-tan lab-like creature hunched in a too-small kennel.

Don't make eye contact, I thought, knowing full well that I would. Soft, gentle, worried eyes met mine, and I was lost. "I'll take him," I heard myself say as I stooped to attach a leash. Stepping back, I was yanked backward by the whirlwind that flew from that kennel. The malamutes had nothing on this guy, and the soft, gentle, worried-eyes thing was probably a figment of my imagination! I was dragged out to my car, and I succeeded in aiming him toward the opened car door before swiftly slamming it shut as his tail disappeared inside. Several minutes were spent in a disagreement about who was to drive, but I persevered and drove us home. I had already named him Emmett by the time I arrived, and I was unceremoniously dragged into the house. Within the first five minutes, Larry and our unlucky house guests were in unanimous agreement—Emmett had not *one* manner. Thus started the huge job of training him to comply with our rules. Amazingly, once he learned that a behaviour was not acceptable, he did not repeat it. I was very thankful that he was such a quick study because he had already impulsively bolted down the road while I was walking him, dragging me over a 20-

foot embankment and landing me waist deep into the lake that he loved. Fortunately, my feet anchored in the rocky lake bottom and hindered him from dragging me farther. He was swimming by that point, and who knows where he was headed!

That week, we started emergency obedience classes. We had several scuffles over his right to attack Chance to establish his leadership in the pack, and we repeatedly informed him that Andi was not interested, that she was spayed. The next week brought an emergency neuter and pitying looks from my colleagues as I took him home the day of his surgery. Still, we were now committed. And we realized that if we didn't get him trained, we would need to *be committed*. Within six months, Emmett became a well-behaved member of our family and attached himself firmly to Larry. He would sit beside Larry's chair, grizzled black and tan head resting on his knee and brown eyes gazing adoringly at Larry. As used to the malamutes as we were—or *by* the malamutes, as it were—this was totally different. Larry looked at Emmett in his usual position one night and said uncomfortably, "You know, I'm not worthy of all this adoration."

Emmett's worst habit—and one that we could not break—was his licking. He would walk past us and, with one swipe of his huge, sticky tongue, wet us from hand to elbow (or worse yet, from neck to eyebrow if we happened to be on his level). Greetings aside, he would lick if we walked past him, if he walked past us, or if we were in his general vicinity. I stopped wearing shorts that summer, and I have not worn them since. We were constantly in need of a towel, and we would automatically greet him with, "Hi, Emmett. Don't lick." In desperation, one day I sprayed my arms with a product called Bitter Apple, which is a foul-tasting liquid applied to surgical sites, wounds, and dressings to prevent dogs from bothering them. *There!* I thought as I deliberately sat on the sofa near him. *See if you like licking now!* His response was unchanged—lick, lick, lick. "You taste funny, Mom," I could almost hear him say. Lick, lick, lick. This went on until I scrambled out of his reach. No amount of discouragement of his habit influenced him at all. "Emmett! Don't lick!" became his name.

As he grew older, he became the benevolent leader of our pack. Rarely did he need to assert himself physically. He maintained his position in the ever-changing pack of rescued dogs (who would stay awhile and then be adopted by new owners) by sheer force of personality. At one point, we had two young, half-grown pups who would often get rowdy and play in the house. One evening, while Emmett rested on his bed in our bedroom, the pups' antics became too much for us. We ordered them to lie down at our feet in the living room. A few minutes later, they were playing roughly again, and we chastised them again. The third time, my voice must have risen. I looked up to see Emmett striding out of our room, directly toward the pups. With steely eyes, he rapidly approached each pup in turn and made a growling mock attack on each one. Those pups separated and found a place to lie down with no repeat of their behaviour. It was as if the head of the household had spoken: "If I have to come out and speak to you again—" Meanwhile, we gazed in open-mouthed admiration.

Emmett was obsessed with his Kong toy, one that he had played with since coming to live with us. No matter how hard or how long we threw the toy, he would hurtle himself after it with no concern for obstacles. And he would come striding back with it, head high, chest thrust out, body wiggling with pride and delight, ready to retrieve again. At the same time, we had a young collie mix named Mick who would retrieve a Kong that was thrown simultaneously with Emmett's. Mick would retrieve it several times, and then he would lie down to watch Emmett. His expression seemed to say, "You don't have to be a lab to retrieve a Kong, but you'd have to be one to keep doing it for that long!"

As testament to Emmett's status in our house, I remember one situation well. One evening, I came home from work and was met by Emmett at the door. Emmett was jumping around, trying to lead me to the food bowls. His face said, "Save a starving dog!" and "Feed me! Feed me!" and his body was trembling with excitement. Quickly removing my coat and boots, I was saying, "Just a minute and I'll feed you. I'll be right there! I'm hurrying! I'm getting your supper!" Solemnly, Larry turned to me and asked, "Do you know what would happen to me if I did that?"

We housed many really fabulous dogs who would otherwise have been killed for lack of room in shelters or lack of interest in saving them. The only one that we considered to be unadoptable was Freeman, whom you have now heard about. The others were terrific, lovable, unique animals whose present owners would not give them up for anything. That we had a hand, however small, in finding great homes for them makes me very proud. That many equally fabulous animals are killed (not *euthanized*) daily across the country because of the uncontrolled breeding of pets is a source of great pain and anger—not only for me, but for most veterinarians and humane societies forced to deal with these poor, unwanted animals.

Chapter 8—The Games People Play

Although we play the usual games with our dogs such as fetch and tag, we have many others that most of them love. Unlike many people, we have named our games so we can convey to each other the games to which each stray is most responsive. They range from such unlikely names as kick the dog to bed mice to monster. Others include where in the world is Larry and git yer feet.

Many people play these games unknowingly with their pets. For example, monster is played by having the owner advance slowly toward the dog, hands held in the air, palms toward the dog, fingers bent, eyes locked onto those of the (calm, playful, well-socialized, and nonaggressive) dog. In the deepest voice possible, the owner then says, "I'm a monster!" after which the dog suddenly turns tail and runs in circles around the owner as the owner tries to catch the delighted dog. This game can be a great time for both humans and dogs. After all, both parties are supremely aware that the savvy dog can never be caught by the bumble-footed monster.

Bed mice is a game played with a submissive dog who can safely be allowed onto the bed without having delusions of grandeur and

71

thinking he or she has now become pack leader. It requires the human to lie on the bed with arm or leg under the blanket. The human then makes movements with toes or fingers to attract the dog's attention. As the dog becomes more and more interested in catching the "mouse" under the blankets, sweeping movements may be made to increase the hunting field to include most of the bed. These sweeping movements also speed the frequency and accuracy of the swift pounce (and the frequency of the "mouse" capture). Potential downsides to this game include the above-mentioned leadership issues as well as bruised fingers or toes, torn blankets, and boredom in particularly bright dogs who are well aware that there is no mouse scent on the bed and therefore no mouse—just a human with a weird sense of humour.

Kick the dog, despite its name, is a favourite with many of my dogs. It was founded one day when back pain prevented me from bending over to play the usual game of tag. In this game, the human makes a sweeping movement with one foot directed at the back end of the dog. The dog then tucks his rear and deftly avoids the foot while quickly returning within reach for a second "kick." I have found that dogs don't mind a sweeping touch to that end, but one must remember to temper enthusiasm and remove any latent hostilities from consciousness to prevent any Freudian accidents. This is a game that we would never play with Freeman.

Where in the world is Larry? is a delightful game requiring some intelligence and desire to please in the dog. While the dog's attention is distracted, Larry hides somewhere in the field. At the proper time, I shout excitedly, "Where's Larry?" At this cue, the dogs all run around the field looking for clues to his whereabouts. In my pack, Mick usually starts to search, and then he sees a squirrel and gazes into the treetops, jumping up on the tree occasionally and forgetting that Larry is lost. In his searching, Miles usually finds a long-lost Kong toy and invites a game of fetch. (Who would have thought—a Border collie obsessed with fetch?) Andi lies on the picnic table, watching, aloof—princesses don't search for people, people search for princesses. Freeman (in a separate run for his own safety) barks incessantly. Seven, with a long-suffering sigh, saunters to the tree behind which Larry has hidden. Her bored expression says, "He's right here. Can I have my treat now?"

Only Emmett is loyal enough and focussed enough to search until his adored Larry is found. We don't know if his search continues out of obligation to Larry, or because he hates it when Larry is out of his sight. Of course, there is always the treat incentive. Emmett always finds Larry and escorts him back to the house, walking smartly by his side, looking up into his face as if to say, "I found ya, Larry. Didn't I, huh? I found ya." He then licks at any available part of Larry—pants, shoes, hands. Proudly, he walks beside his favourite person, head up, tail wagging, eyes constantly checking for Larry's gaze. Watching Emmett with Larry never fails to make me smile.

Chapter 9—DunRoamin'

I n the early years at my clinic, we saw many strays, cats picked up off the road, dogs hit by cars, kittens thrown into the woods, starving animals found in remote areas where they would never go on their own. Emotionally, I was ill-equipped to refuse them care or kill them. I didn't go to vet school to kill animals. A couple of days on intravenous fluids, a few antibiotics, some good food and proper care and warmth, and she'd be fine. A splint, a few weeks in a kennel, and he'd be fine. A few sutures, a neuter, some antibiotics, and he'd be okay. It always seems like very small interventions can save animals. Admittedly, there were strays that I couldn't save. I euthanized some but consoled myself with the idea that they had died warm, pain free, and with someone who cared.

We had many, many kittens abandoned in the woods—thrown out in the garbage or left in boxes at the roadside. Larry, Janice, and I did our best for the little ones, and we badgered our families and friends to provide homes for them. We covered treatment costs ourselves. Most of the kittens we received were sick with one of several feline viruses, which caused infected eyes, sneezing, and upper respiratory problems. They were the little, boney, starved waifs with red, sore eyes. They were crawling with fleas, and their ears were filled with debris from ear mites. They came from the worst homes. With great medical precision, we termed these *scuzzy kittens*. And we did our best for them. Soon, clients became aware of our little sideline, and they began to donate toward the cost of medications and surgeries. Others stepped forward to offer foster homes while the strays were healing. We could not express our appreciation adequately! About that time, my sister, Martha, moved home. She didn't have any pets. In no time flat, she acquired six cats.

One afternoon, a well-dressed client, Susan, stopped in with a kitten that her sister had picked up off the road. This was one of the scuzziest kittens that I had ever seen: nothing but bones, eyes gummed shut with green secretions, struggling to breathe through clogged nostrils, weak, and covered with fleas.

"Thank you for bringing him in," I said, taking his little body in my arms and starting directly for the treatment room.

"Wait!" Susan called. "Who pays for all the treatment this kitten needs?"

"We do," I replied, "with help from donations from clients."

"That's not right," she insisted. "You shouldn't have to pay for all the community's strays." As we kept her updated on the kitten's condition, Susan made plans. One day, she announced, "I'm going to help raise funds to cover costs!"

With that, DunRoamin' Stray and Rescue was born. (We often need to explain that when strays come to us, they are all "done roamin'.") Under Susan's direction, funds were raised that even allowed us to send animals to a nearby animal hospital for orthopaedic surgical repairs.

Going a large step further, Susan started a website, www. bekindtogodscreatures.com. My sister, Martha, had started chronicling the story of each stray or rescue, and she displayed the stories along with pictures of each animal in an album. Clients checked the album on each visit to the clinic, and they often left with a new family member. Collaboratively, the two of them kept the website up to date, adding in advice on spaying and neutering and many other topics.

When Dr. Shannon Monteith joined the clinic, I was delighted to have found a like-minded associate. Like me, she often had a houseful: kittens with broken legs, kittens who needed feeding every four hours, kittens who had lost an eye or had some other serious illnesses. As great as she was with all the strays, she loved the babies. That worked well because I loved the adults—although I was occasionally surprised with a few litters of puppies from recently rescued dogs.

It was a common sight to see Shannon arrive at the clinic in the morning with a dog wearing a cast or splint and a cat carrier filled with tiny orphaned kittens. And then she would return to her vehicle to bring in another needy animal. When this happened, we knew that she was on call and couldn't count on getting home. She had brought her rescues and her own two dogs—one of which was an 18-year-old beagle from the veterinary teaching hospital where we trained.

There are some people who seem to attract the unexpected, but Shannon attracted the weird stuff! One morning, she came to work carrying what appeared to be an infant dog, umbilical cord still attached. Someone had found the small canid on their driveway in the night and contacted the vet on call, Shannon. Speculation ran rampant. Could it be a Pekinese pup, a shepherd mix, a weird-looking mixed breed? Devotedly, she fed and looked after her tiny charge, whose appearance sparked more and more speculation. Soon, even Shannon had to agree that it wasn't like any pup she'd ever seen. It could outrun her and jump seemingly impossible heights at less than five weeks of age. Familiar with my puppies, I knew that they would still be waddling unsteadily at that stage and grunting *nnnuf, nnnuf* when they were picked up. This little one was starting to growl and bite. Through the wonders of the Internet, we were able to compare photos of various wild canid pups until we identified it as a coyote. Luckily, we were able to get the increasingly less cuddly pup to a wildlife rehabilitation centre where she would be raised to return to the wild.

Our strays increased in number as people heard about our interest in helping them. We had to defend ourselves from many who tried to use the clinic as a drop-off for unwanted pets. We began using each venue available to try to educate and promote spays and neuters. We felt that our mandate was to assist the animals who would fall through the cracks—those too sick to be handled by the shelters, too costly to be paid for by the shelters, too young to go there, and so on. Still, we often found packages on our doorstep in the morning—a pup and an irate cat stuffed together into a small cat carrier, a tiny kitten in the middle of the driveway, two empty boxes with a note saying, "We are all litter trained." (We hope we found them all—the poor, boney, flea-infested little things.)

Busier and busier with our little street friends—and with our veterinary clinic growing markedly busier as well—I wasn't surprised when Shannon arrived at work one morning with another tiny scrap of dog-dom. Its umbilical cord was still attached, and she had found it on the sidewalk in the middle of town. Its unfamiliar appearance restarted the speculation that she had another coyote.

"Like that could ever happen twice!" she laughed, and she put away the tiny nursing bottle to attend to clients. As time passed, though, even Shannon had to admit that it wasn't your regular, run-of-the-mill pup. In fact, it wasn't a pup at all, we eventually confirmed! It was a cub, a fox cub! The wildlife rehab had closed, and we could not find a place for this little one to go. We got advice from different professionals on raising the cub to return to the wild. We all stopped hugging the little fox—no loss for him because he was starting to hate it. We were instructed to introduce him to the foods that he would have to forage for and hunt in the wild. There was no problem buying the little guy different kinds of berries and apples, but to serve him mice? Amazingly, our clients came through for us again, chasing down their own cats and robbing them of the spoils of the hunt. They would drop off the mice at our clinic. One lady even went so far as to freeze the mice caught by her cats and deliver them to the clinic all frozen and packaged! Crickets and mealworms were also required, and we left that duty to Shannon. The fox lived in an overgrown, outside cat run where he could be safely exposed to the outdoors and yet avoid traffic and other dangers. Finally, he was deemed old enough to survive on his own, and he was driven to a remote area where Shannon's friend had a cottage and was willing to supplement food for the remainder of the summer. Released, he never looked back (the ingrate!). But I like to think that he found a girlfriend and lived a wild life as he was meant to.

There were so many strays—too many to mention—and yet we got not only the great feeling of having helped another living being but also the fun opportunity to name them. They were given short-term names, knowing that new owners would surely choose something else. There was Garth, the huge tomcat; Truman, the gentle giant of a dog; Easy, the pitbull/lab cross who was anything but; Fanta and Nesbitt, the orange cats (remember those brands of orange pop?);

there was Forrest who was found, well, in the forest; Wednesday Addams, the kitten who was thrown from a car and sustained facial and upper lip injuries; and little Mayday, found in big trouble on the first day of May. Then there was the final capture of a litter of wild sheltie pups, a little girl named Lastlie! The perfect cat names, such as Purrl, Furlin, Katya, Willya, Ferris Mewler, and Purrcilla were always doled out eagerly. I love naming! The next time we admit an extremely matted, long-haired cat that needs to have his entire coat clipped, I have a name all picked out. I think I'll call him Bare. (or if he's white, I may call him Dwhite).

DunRoamin' has grown far larger than I ever imagined. Although we don't have a shelter building, we have what I like to call an extramural shelter. Our strays, for the most part, are living in loving foster homes, receiving the care they need, and learning to be good pets. DunRoamin' supporters donate money, goods, crafts to sell, and items to raffle. They take scuzzy kittens home, clean and nurse them, and bring back healthy pets, ready to be adopted. They man tables at craft sales, yard sales, and bake sales. They walk their adopted dogs in the Florenceville-Bristol Canada Day parade (in what we call the DunRoamin' Mutt Strutt), proud to share with any onlooker the obstacles that each dog has overcome to find his rightful home. They donate food and dog beds and cat kennels. They visit the clinic basement weekly to cuddle and socialize the dozen or so cats constantly in residence there. They drive the animals to their medical appointments with us. One cat, Itchy, was driven to the Atlantic Veterinary College in Prince Edward Island—a six-hour drive—for a specialist consultation. (He needed to see a dermatologist because he was, well, itchy.) They build dog houses and insulated cat boxes for feral cats and make sure the feral cats are fed. They knit warm cat beds and have open houses or garden tours with donations accepted for DunRoamin'. They even give talks to school children, Scout, Cub, or Guide groups on animal care, and they impress the very urgent need for pets to be spayed or neutered on anyone who will listen. Children have donated their allowances or asked that, instead of birthday gifts, necessities be donated for the strays. They even write articles for us to help fulfill our obligations for our weekly newspaper column, "We're All DunRoamin'" in the local paper, *The Bugle-Observer*. We really are all DunRoamin', and as our website points out: "We made a difference for that one!"

Chapter 10—Buddy

Not long ago, I received information that the local shelter had taken in a thirteen-and-a-half-year-old large breed dog. To say that I was annoyed is an understatement. I was incensed! I had heard that his elderly owners were not available to look after him due to death or the need to move to a nursing home. Still, I could not get this unseen old dog off my mind. I described to everyone the resulting consequences if, on my demise, my old animals were sent to a shelter. And I quote, "If I died and none of my friends or family would take in my old animals—forcing them to end up in a shelter—I would come back and haunt them all!" After contemplating that threat, my brother John commented that as objects flew around the room and ghostly noises filled the house, my family would simply shrug and say, "Oh, it's just Moon again." (*Moon* is my family's nickname for me). My irritation regarding this dog's plight is in no way a criticism of shelters. They do the best they can in a world where people often do not spay or neuter, or view pets as disposable. No, this anger came from someone's willingness to discard someone else's old friend. It came from the lack of concern and compassion and the fact that no one would step up and look after the dog for the short time he had left.

Just knowing he was there haunted me for several days until I was informed that he would be euthanized—he was leaving messes throughout the facility. (He was, it should be noted, allowed out with the staff in an attempt to give him more attention and love.) Shannon, who often donated her time at the shelter, agreed to bring him back with her the next day.

Preparations were made. He could sleep at night in our largest crate in the living room. I could drive the short distance home at noon to let him out. He could stay in our house with our other very old dog, Andi. It would work.

The next day, Shannon arrived with a very large, very stiff old dog named Buddy. She lifted him from her vehicle and set him on unsteady legs on the ground beside her. He looked around, confused and a little frightened. His black, wiry hair whitened around his eyes and muzzle, his tail hung down, his eyes opened wide. As he took his first stiff, tentative steps toward me in response to my welcoming call and use of his name, I started a mental checklist of concerns and necessary medications—omega-3 fatty acids, glucosamine, analgesics for his stiff legs, an eye exam (was that left pupil dilated and fixed?), a physical exam (I'd heard he had a heart murmur), and screening blood work (may as well know what I'm dealing with). And then I started trying to win a place in his heart. I had no knowledge of his life or his people. If he was to live happily with us, he needed to bond with and learn to trust Larry and me. We needed to become his people—and quickly because I wondered whether he would live six more months.

It wasn't that we felt that he desperately needed to live longer. There are worse things than death for an old companion animal, but we felt that he should not die discarded, frightened, bewildered, and wondering why his people were not there with him. We did not intend to extend his life, just to return to him his dignity, security, and feeling of love and belonging. And then we would allow him to go peacefully when he was ready—with family present to see him off. As it turned out, after Buddy learned that we were okay, we were the ones who gained much from knowing him. We never failed to laugh when he barked at us to share our food. His front feet lifted from the floor with each bark, the tone more and more demanding with each bark. His tolerance of the foster pups made us smile. One small pup who had been found in a deep snow bank in a rural area desperately attached himself to Buddy. The pup's rescuer had called for help for this freezing little guy, and when asked how big the pup was, he had replied, "Oh, about the size of a football!" Little Tony found Buddy to be not only soft and warm, but also secure. Buddy always tolerated the pup's very close proximity, but he looked at us as if to say, "Get it off me!"

It was February, and the snow at our house had blown into high drifts. Buddy was not interested in doing his business while on a leash, and another finding: he was deaf and could only hear loud, high notes (ones Larry was not capable of producing). In the safety of our yard, Larry would release him from the leash and wait until he was ready to come in. Time after time, I would be unable to restrain my laughter as Bud would head for the deep drifts from which he was unable to extricate himself. This left Larry no choice but to wade into the drifts, usually in his slippers, to carry the big guy back to the plowed driveway. I would hear, in a falsetto rivalling that of Barry Gibbs, "Buddy, no! No, no!" (with each *no* a little higher than the last). "Buddy, Buddy, *Buddy!* Oh, shit!" I would hear him yell. I would know without looking that he had run off into the deep snow and was stuck up to his sides in the deep drifts. Larry was his only hope of "Stayin' Alive." The choice of swear words often gave me a hint regarding his choice of footwear that night.

With attention—and following the lead of the other dogs—Buddy settled in with us and began to flourish. He soon understood that the softest dog beds were the first occupied, so upon returning from his nightly walk, he would rush to the best bed. He would then stare defiantly at the younger, more resilient dogs as if to say, "I need this more than you do!"

Buddy lived in the house with Andi, who was of similar vintage and just as hard of hearing. It made me laugh to hear Larry shout for help when he had taken the two old dogs out for bathroom duties. They would be tottering off in different directions, one toward the road, one out over the hill. I would always shout for Buddy because he could hear the pitch of my voice—even when momentum was carrying him toward the foot of our steep driveway. "Buddy, come back here! I'm the one who loves you!"

Meanwhile, Larry would have to run out over the hill after Andi. He would tap her on the shoulder and indicate with hand signals that she needed to go home with him. I always suspected both dogs of having better hearing than we thought because I could never get a crinkle-wrapped treat open without them both appearing at my side.

Buddy soon became a favourite with guests because he greeted them with warm attention and excess drool that usually accumulated in his jowls and dribbled out when he rested his head in their laps. He was a social bully, staring guests in the eye and barking constantly to obtain his share of their meals. We allowed this behaviour in Buddy, but not in our other dogs. After all, he was deaf and old and partially blind—and he had a heart murmur. Who knows whether his previous life was one of comfort and love, or whether he was tied in the backyard all the time—and besides, how long would he live?

A year later, a friend asked me whether we still had that great, old black dog—the one whose front legs lifted from the floor each time he barked, the one who demanded food from everyone. We did, and he still got his own way with the barking—but the front legs didn't lift as far off the floor now, and it was much more difficult for him to get around (even with the ramps that we had installed for him).

Larry and I worried constantly that he was in too much pain because his arthritis was much worse. We had changed his medications many times to try to keep him comfortable. Still, he demanded his share of my meals (his share kept getting larger and larger), and he continued to play some little games that we had devised for him. He didn't have to stand or move to play these games (such as get your whiskers). Arthritis was not a factor. Often, he initiated the games and was certainly the first and most ardent greeter of guests. We told ourselves that Buddy would tell us when he was ready to leave, when he had had enough.

One year and one month after he came to live with us, Buddy asked to go. He hadn't bothered to greet guests the day before, and he had left half of my breakfast unfinished that morning. He had to be carried outside, and he was relieved to be placed back on his bed when he finished. The expression in his eyes said, "I hurt, and I'm ready." We had no doubts. We let him go gently and quietly on the softest dog bed, surrounded by Andi, his other friends, Larry, and me. We all loved him.

Chapter 11—The Pups, More or Less

Whoever said, "No good deed goes unpunished" was right on the mark. We are the perfect examples. We also personify the old adage, "Some people never learn"—and yet, it is what we do. We try to help strays and other pets in trouble. Our house has been temporary quarters to a great long list of dogs in trouble—dogs who were to be shot, pups found in the woods or in a snow bank or in a garbage bag, dogs who lay for hours after being hit by vehicles, dogs who were found shot, dogs who had never seen the inside of a house, starving dogs who whelped a litter on arrival, and on and on. A discerning visitor would note evidence of the high turnover of dogs and pups in our house. By that I mean the corner was chewed off the woodwork there, teeth marks were visible on the rungs of that chair, scratch marks were on the windowsills, there was no cloth cover on the bottom of our box spring, there were multiple, deep tooth impressions on the base of the dining room table, and we had no screen doors. We used to have screen doors, but we just couldn't seem to keep screens on them. The flies aren't that bad, anyway.

One thing that I do enjoy—second to the dogs—is the group of flowers that I plant in containers (for obvious reasons) and the

Virginia creeper that has finally reached the top of our pergola, making a thick cover over it.

Last year, the container garden on our front deck had reached its peak. Every pot was filled with brightly blooming plants. I could see them from almost every spot in the living room and kitchen, and coupled with the Virginia creeper, it felt like my own little oasis right there on the deck. We received a message from a client that a neighbour was about to shoot three dogs who were the offspring of his very fertile and unspayed female. At our request, she obtained permission to bring the pups to us. She arrived shortly with two three-month-old golden-coloured pups and their nine-month-old black and brindle brother.

It was easy to see that these little guys had had little handling, and I doubted they had ever been in the house. After vaccinating and deworming them, I brought them home. I was appalled at how frightened they seemed.

I won't force them, I thought, *I'll let them into the small pen at the front of the house that includes the deck and let Easy in with them to demonstrate that there is nothing to fear.* Easy was another stray who had lived with us for six months, and she loved to play with puppies. She was also very confident and loving, and I thought she would make a great role model.

Because it was hot, and Easy loved the water, I had filled a child's blue wading pool with water and placed it just outside the French doors. That way, I knew I didn't have to worry about their hydration. I anticipated seeing her cool herself by sitting in the water and perhaps splashing somewhat as she usually did.

Releasing the pups and Easy into the pen, I watched to see if there would be any problems. When the pups seemed to settle and Easy seemed happy, I ran to the laundry room to try to catch up on some housework. As the day wore on, the pups began to feel more comfortable, following Easy into the house and gradually submitting to more and more petting. I wanted to name the young male Morley, so that left me no choice but to name his sister Leslie. The older pup I named Regis. Gradually, through closer contact, I realized that Leslie was actually larger than Morley, giving credence to the expression "Les is More."

Finally, after a few hours, all three pups were settled, happy, and beginning to play while I was in the room.

Great, I thought as I went back to the laundry room to finish the giant mound of unironed clothes, swatting at the deer flies and mosquitoes that had availed themselves of that one small door. *Socializing them shouldn't be too bad.* I thought. Each minute seemed to bring more and more normal behaviour, and soon they were all running to me for hugs and petting. A short time later, I caught a glimpse of my reflection in the bathroom mirror. Trailed by four tail-wagging dogs, I wondered at the brown stains on my face. As I washed them off, I saw with relief that it was only mud, and I smiled at the thought of dogs being dogs. I finished the huge pile of laundry, occasionally wondering at the faint sound of water running.

I returned to the living room and gasped as Morley darted through the French doors, four feet of Virginia creeper trailing behind him. Leslie was a close second, biting at the ends of his leafy cape. The deck was covered with planting soil, and Easy was rolling poor Regis in the mud. My heart stopped at the sight of bright red splotches all over the deck, but then I realized that it was just the remains of my favourite, ever-blooming, bright red ivy geranium—not blood. The floor around the doors was covered with muddied water, and the pups raced through the "great blue water bowl," splashing even more water into the house. The living room was littered with the remnants of my garden, and the distorted clumps of my lobelia suggested that many a tug of war had taken place. Plants floated in the blue wading pool, and skeletons of my leafy pride and joy lay scattered throughout the pen. Mor and Les were having the time of their lives, and only Easy had the grace to look worried as I sighed loudly. Her unsettled expression and the concern in her soft brown eyes did little to appease me—what with her mud-spattered body and sprigs of my favourite pansies still dangling from her teeth. After several deep breaths, I called a meeting with all four dogs on the mud-spattered deck.

The pups' eyes sparkled as they poked at each other and splashed in the great blue water bowl. All three were totally soaked, panting, and completely oblivious to my state of mind. Easy, however, maintained a perfect heel position, sitting immediately whenever I stopped. As I stood there looking down at her, I noticed that she had spit out the pansies. She still looked worried. With steely control, I spoke calmly to her: "Go get your ball." Her eyes sparkled, and she leapt over one puppy and off the deck, returning immediately to offer me a slippery, muddy Kong toy. Through gritted teeth and in dulcet tones, I praised her. "Good girl, you rotten, miserable guttersnipe!" She relaxed to play with her friends again.

Later that evening as Larry and I sat on the deck—four tired and wet dogs at our feet, a mat of wilting Virginia creeper covering the pergola (yep, chewed off at the base), and flies and mosquitoes swarming us (there was no sense going indoors)—we wondered if there could perhaps have been a better way to handle this group. I took the Easy way out—I said it was all her fault.

However, in the future, we've decided to monitor our newcomers much more closely and make more use of the several empty runs when we are busy. Maybe I'll place my container garden on the back patio this year.

Not all of our contacts with our rescued dogs are as traumatic. One shepherd/collie-cross, Midas, an extremely active and intelligent fellow who had spent too long in a shelter, came to us via Shannon. The shelter had called, and they were becoming concerned about his behaviour. They felt that he was becoming aggressive. Confined and restless as he was, they wondered if he would need to be euthanized for the protection of staff and visitors. She brought him to work, and I was immediately smitten.

"I'll take him home and look after him for the day," I said, surprising both Shannon and myself. Midas and I walked the kilometre to my house, and we were stopped by my brother, Dave, who was also taken with his appearance. While we discussed and admired him, Midas's behaviour was exemplary. I couldn't help but think that Dave's farm might be the place for him—there would be plenty of activity to keep him interested.

We continued our walk, and upon arrival at my home, I watched with a smile as he did not show aggression toward my dogs. Next, we went into the house where I released him and sat down to enjoy a coffee. Midas came to me and rested his head on my knee. More as a test of his temperament than anything, I lifted him into my lap. To my surprise, he immediately relaxed, put his head on my shoulder, and seemed to try to glue himself to me as I wrapped both arms around him. For almost an hour, I sat with that beautiful dog on my lap. The only way I have of describing how I felt is to say that he was absorbing much-needed love and comfort from me. Fine by me! I live to serve!

Midas was adopted by my brother, and he has settled in very nicely. The behaviours that so concerned the shelter staff disappeared and were, I think, the result of boredom and frustration—a problem that is often seen in shelters, no matter how hard the shelter staff tries. I see him frequently, racing in the fields as Dave checks on his cattle, expending that long pent-up energy, and enjoying his life as a happy and well-loved farm dog. That is not to say that everyone could have handled a dog such as Midas—he is not an easy dog—but his family is totally committed to him; his family is attentive to his quirks and keeps him out of trouble.

Chapter 12—Those Darn Cats

Although we had many stray and rescued dogs at our house, we were not able to bring cats home because some of the dogs were potential cat killers. Still, the number of stray, starving, injured, and abused cats brought to the clinic was several times that of the dogs. I could not ignore this terrible situation. My only choice was to establish a small area in the basement of the clinic for recovered cats and harass my best clients to adopt or assist with finding adoptive homes. My clients came through in an amazing way. They, their friends, and their families kept the numbers of cats at the clinic at a manageable level.

One morning, as I was driving into town, I spotted two tiny kittens in the middle of the road—one white and one black. Appalled, I stopped to pick them up and returned home. They were barely old enough to eat, and they were very cold. I took them into the house, warmed them up, and fed them kitten milk replacer from tiny nursing bottles. I then set them up in what I considered to be quite luxurious surroundings in my laundry room. They had a padded laundry basket, hot water bottles, a stuffed bear for cuddling, and a good solid door between them and the dogs. Each time I fed them, which was every three or four hours, I locked all the dogs away and allowed the kittens to climb and play on me as I sat on the sofa or lay on the bed.

After two days, Larry said to me, "You know, if these had been puppies, they would have been named within five minutes of coming into the house. These poor kittens don't even have names!"

Defensively, I told him that they did have names. And when asked what their names were, I sputtered, "Their names are ... are ... Frank and Richard!" (Those were the first names that had come into my head.) When Larry immediately asked which was which, I was ready for him. "The white one is Richard!" Later that day, my sister, Martha, and her friend stormed into my house like avenging angels. They proclaimed my house full of dogs an unfit place to raise kittens and my allotment of time to the kittens woefully inadequate. As rabid cat people, both were appalled when a cat's tiny feet had to touch a hard surface or a cat had only one bed in which to lounge. They packed up one black and one white tiny body and the milk replacer and food—but they refused to use my clothes basket and hot water bottles.

"We'll bring them back when they are ready for new homes," they said. They left me chastened and secretly relieved to get back to my dogs. Don't get me wrong, I love cats and feel very strongly about their care and about the prevention of cat suffering (which is so epidemic it's obscene). My heart breaks when I see the traumas these little guys suffer—the starvation, the fear, and the homelessness. Still, when I come home, I like someone to greet me as if I were the most important person in the world—instead of the other way around.

Our clients began notifying us if they saw a cat in trouble, and they often went to great lengths to help them or bring them in for treatment. One of our favourite clients, Marie, had told me several times about a tomcat that she was feeding but could not touch. Her major concern for him was that she saw him so often on the road, and she was afraid he would be killed. Each phone conversation with her ended with her saying something like, "He's on the road again, and he's going to be killed!" Still, he seemed to be coping with her help. One day, however, Marie called to tell us that he was injured. His face was so infected that he couldn't eat. She lived nearby, so we went to her house and were able to catch him (she had already trapped him in her garage). The big grey-and-white tom bore the marks of repeated brawling. He had somewhat tattered ear tips and old scars on his face. He also had multiple new and infected bite wounds from fighting, and his face was grotesquely swollen. We returned to the clinic with him where he was treated and neutered and found to be quite a cuddle cat, purring and kneading with his front feet when patted. Since he had long grey hair, loved his weed (our name for catnip), and had always been "on the road again," we decided that he should be called Willie Nelson. He settled into clinic life easily, but many predicted that, as an indoor cat, he'd be crazy.

Not long after accepting Willie, Martha was feeding cats at the nearby farm late in the evening when she heard the sounds of a cat in distress. It was crying—wailing, actually—and following the beam of her flashlight, she finally made out the form of a black cat. As she bent to pick him up, she saw that his whole side was scraped and infected, and that he was terribly thin. I was called to meet her at the clinic for examination and treatment. I guessed that his injury was probably a road rash, that he had been hit or dragged by a car. By this time, tradition had it that all admissions needed to be named on the spot. And it seemed that, since we already had Willie, this new cat must be Wailin'. He submitted to my ministering with good humour, and before long, he was serenading us with his deep, purring songs.

Wailin' was another example of the filthy old street cat who was struggling to survive (and bearing wounds as testament to the difficulties of street living). He was exhausted by the constant struggle to survive and the need for continual vigilance. Fed and rested, he cleaned himself up and showed himself to be a gentle and loving personality. And some months later, he fell in love with another street waif, a calico named Callie. From the moment they met, they became a team and were never apart. We decided that they must be adopted together or stay (together) with us. After some time, Wailin' and Callie got the great home they deserved. Our staff was satisfied—they had a wonderful, safe home, and they were together. We love happy endings!

With the addition of Wailin' to our group, it struck me that we were in a most unique situation. Frank and Richard—half-grown by now and living at the clinic—were often referred to as "the boys." So darned if we didn't have Willie and Wailin' and The Boys right there in our own building. Starstruck, I informed everyone who would listen. And then it occurred to me that there must be a country song in this situation. Perhaps it would go something like:

Me and the boys got road rashes,
We'll need a place to scatter our ashes,
If we don't stay off that dangerous highway,
We'll be looking down from the heavenly skyway,
Singin' road rashes, road rashes,
We all got road rashes …

Purely as an intellectual exercise, I wondered to myself what we would have named these cats if, during our country singer phase, they had both been female. And then, I knew: Anne Purray and Kit D Lang! And their song? "Slow Bird," of course!

The cats that we often see—collected from the road or abandoned in some barn where "there are lots of mice to live on"—come to us in terrible shape. They are starved, sick, parasitized, infected, and injured. We name them immediately. No one should die without a name! At one point, we were trying to make a point with the names that we chose because we knew their plight would be described in our column in the local paper.

Two kittens came to us one day. They were sick with high fevers, infected eyes, and severe respiratory infections—all aggravated by their abysmal physical condition. They were filthy and starving, struggling to breathe. They were very close to death, cold, and unable to stand. Emergency intervention and treatment gradually improved their conditions until they started to show signs that they might survive. After several days, they became interested in their appearances, and they began spending hours grooming, primping, and preening. They wanted to look their best. Soon, they were immaculate and looking quite princely. Each day saw them looking and acting better and better, until I realized that, despite what the world had done to them, they were still wonders of design. Their little faces, their green eyes, their beautiful orange coats—they were all the work of a master of composition, a designer of immense and unparalleled talent.

With continued loving care, their coats will just get better and better. They'll shine, glistening in the sun, as they were meant to. They are special, each of those kittens—one of a kind. With coats like that, we know they're not knock-offs! They're Armani and Versace! Those little guys went on to get the great homes that they deserved. Perhaps their suffering was worth it in the end.

Chapter 13—The Diva

We saw many, many animals rescued from the streets or in need of our help. Some we accepted from owners who, for whatever reason, would not be willing to bear the costs of treatment or the time commitment required to treat and convalesce their animals. If they elected to put the animal down, we would ask for ownership of any that we felt were salvageable. We found it easier to commit our time and skills to fix those who were fixable and then find homes for them.

All the rescues were certainly worthy of our care, and they were eventually adopted into loving homes. Some I remember more clearly than others, though, as if we had somehow connected in a different way. There are those that I will never forget—some due to the rampant destruction they inflicted on our home and our lives, and others just because we connected somehow.

One dog that I will never forget was a young golden retriever, a mere pup of eight months found by her owners lying in a ditch. She had been hit by a car sometime earlier in the day. She was brought to the clinic with extensive injuries. She was in shock but fairly alert. She was unable to stand due to obvious injuries to at least three of her legs, and she was bloody and dishevelled. She smelled of urine, and she was coated with gravel. When informed of the injuries, her owner opted to put her down. She was badly injured with a dislocated elbow, dislocated hip, multiple pelvic fractures, and a huge laceration to her mouth that allowed her nose to move upward and sideways by more than an inch.

Shannon was on duty and asked my opinion as to whether she was a DunRoamin' candidate. Should we take her on given her severe injuries and the very costly treatment and lengthy convalescence required? Would we be doing her any favours to put her through such an extensive and difficult treatment and recovery? As we stood there beside the exam table where she lay quietly, Shannon lowered her head near the dog's face and was rewarded with a huge, bloody lick that extended from her neck to her forehead. Smiling at each other, we said, "We'd better get to work."

We started with pain control and shock treatment, and then we graduated to X-rays and wound management. When she was stable, we reduced her dislocations, strapped them into position to heal for two to three weeks, repaired her terrible nose injury, and removed her broken teeth.

After multiple surgeries, we had repaired as much as we could. The rest was up to the dog—now called Diva. She needed several weeks of total rest before we would even consider letting her try to walk. She moved in with Larry and me for about 7 weeks to allow all those fractures to heal. She was confined in a small area, and she was not allowed to walk, run, or play. What about all that energy? What about the total lack of training and manners?

Thankfully, Diva was able to amuse herself. A friend had left a large bag of toys for our constant stream of strays, and a recent gift was a squeaky toy made in the form of a child's jack (six arms projecting from the round, central area). Each arm was a squeaker—the centre, a louder squeaker. The first week, as she lay on her side (unable to even turn herself), she moved her hind foot, accidentally kicking the toy and causing a squeak. Lifting her head to see the source of the noise, to our delight, she kicked the toy again. We became less and less thrilled as she entertained herself over the next hour, constantly kicking at the toy still wedged in her blankets near her feet.

When she was due to be turned on her other side, I foolishly handed her the toy. She spent the next interminable hour alternately biting it, bumping it with her nose, hitting it with her one good leg, and rolling her head on it. She was delighted with its shrieks each time she struck it, and very little could distract her. She took breaks for short periods for meals, chew toys, visits from her friends, and to be carried outside for bathroom breaks. But she always returned to her squeaky toy, from which she could now elicit three or four differently pitched squawks simultaneously. Happy to see her occupied and relaxed in her infirmity (although we were almost insane with the constant squeaks), I neglected to remove the toy at bedtime. Instead, a very disgruntled Larry snatched it from her bed around 3 a.m. when its shrieks, squeaks, screams, and squawks awakened us from a deep sleep. Fuzzily, I recalled the afternoon's cacophony of similar noises, and gradually and with relief, I recognized the sounds of Diva's toy. The relief we felt at not having a murderous attack occurring in our house in the dead of the night was enormous. Lesson learned: remove *that* toy from Diva's bed at our bedtime.

As fate would have it, a few days after Diva moved in with us, I fell and fractured my ankle. Larry, whose workload had markedly increased, struggled (with good cheer) to look after all of us. He would settle me into the lounger in the backyard, return to the house, and carry Diva to a bed placed next to it so that we could enjoy the sun and the outdoors. Diva, disagreeing with his arrangements, used all her strength to climb onto the lounger with me, body between my legs, head and neck resting on my chest and abdomen. We both had a short nap to recover from our exertions, but then Diva began to check out my face and arms. Could that be remnants of ice cream there on your face? Is that a boo-boo on your arm? Still have a little gravy on your fingers? Is that a bird flying up there? Need your nose cleaned? My, your hair smells good! What's that metal around your neck? Want me to chew it off for you? Should I chew your fingernails a little shorter?

In an effort to entertain her, I started a common game where I pretended that I was going to grab her left ear with my right hand as she faced me. Slowly, I move my hand toward her ear as she watches in excited anticipation. Should that hand grab her, she would try to grab me before I could pull it away (making her the winner).

After a few tries where I narrowly missed being grabbed, I altered my game plan. Slowly, I edged my right hand toward her left ear. As the tension mounted, her eyes sparkled with anticipation. Suddenly, I grabbed her right ear with my left hand, leaving my right hand still in attack position. Diva was incensed! "Cheater!" her face told me. She barked and growled repeatedly at me, mouthing both my hands as her tail wagged with glee.

Now, new rules: both hands in attack position. Which would she need to fend off? Enjoying this as much as Diva—observing the delight in her eyes and her wagging tail—I watched her concentrate, alert for the slightest movement, the slightest indicator of my intent. Perhaps I watched too long, entranced by her response to the game. Her expression said, "I'm watching you! You won't surprise me again!

I know your tactics!" Her eyes moved from hand to hand. "I'm faster than you are! You won't get me again! Fool me once, shame on you! Fool me twice—oh, a mosquito!" She forgot her game with wonder in her eyes as her head bobbed and tracked the erratic path of the insect. With the mosquito gone, she returned her attention to me. She glanced questioningly at my hands (still in attack position), and with a faint *chuff,* she gave me a look that I'd seen many times on the faces of my older brothers. That look clearly said, "Oh, grow up!" With a deep sigh, she rested her head again on my chest and fell asleep, leaving me awake and feeling a little silly as I affectionately stroked her blonde head.

As she recovered, her pain subsided. She was now bored with everything except her favourite toy. It was easy to see that, wisely or not, Diva wanted to run. We put her in a large wire exercise pen with plenty of room to stand, move around, and stretch. She had no chance of damaging her still fragile bone repairs. In attempts to draw my attention to her boredom, she would lie in her pen and stare at me (lying, foot elevated, on the sofa). It always made me smile to see how she rested her now-healed nose on the transverse wire of the pen—just the upper black part—with her lower jaw hanging open. One afternoon, when it was almost time for Larry to carry her outside, I glanced up when I heard a sigh from her. I saw Diva with her nose resting as usual on the transverse wire, but she was applying so much weight that all her front incisors and long canine teeth were in full view—like a huge, bored snarl. When I burst out laughing, her expression just said, "Wha'?"

Gradually, she was allowed out of the pen for short walks around the house. Fearing that she might start wrestling with the other dogs, I made sure they were all outside. That left only our very grouchy, "don't mess with me" 14-year-old Andi in the house with Diva. At her first attempt to sniff Andi, she was met with an intolerant "Back off!" bark. Her eyes lit up, and her tail began to wag furiously. Like some monstrous eight-week-old puppy, Diva poked Andi with her nose and easily dodged the bared fang (a terrible parody of a vicious threat made all the more gruesome by the empty gums, the glimpse of the occasional molar, and the fierce glint in Andi's bluish eye). And so it went on: Poke! Bark! Growl! Dart! Wag! After a few minutes, the Diva was returned to her pen for bad behaviour, and Andi retired to her bed, secure in the knowledge that she had bested yet another young pup.

Diva, now healed and healthy, lives happily with a family who is working on teaching her acceptable manners. They had contacted me when they saw pictures of Diva on our DunRoamin' website. The family had originally agreed to get a little dog, but the mother of two young children said that she couldn't get Diva's face out of her mind after seeing the pictures. One meeting with Diva and they were sold. Diva's new owner said that it was Diva's love of life—and her strong sense that the dog wanted to enjoy the life that she had been given—that drew her to the injured pup. They say that she is a work in progress (regarding her manners), but now that she is able to run to her heart's content, she is behaving better. A good dog is a tired dog. Diva has come a long way to reach her rightful place in this world—from broken ditch dog to cherished pet.

Diva is amazing. She is incorrigible, full of life, playful, smart, funny, annoying, and (at times) incredibly dumb. We are better people for having known her. We will always remember her innate and total goodness, love of life, will to live, and hysterical behaviours.

Chapter 14—When Harry Met Mil

"I wish you could meet Harry! He's the teenaged Border collie picked up at large by the SPCA and brought to our clinic. He had obviously been attacked by another dog because the entire right side of his head and neck was torn and bruised, and the bite wounds were badly infected. He was in a lot of pain. It was also emotionally painful for me to touch him—he was nothing but bones.

"Veterinary clinic staff spent two hours combing him out under anaesthesia (his coat was one terrible mat) while Shannon attended to his horrific wounds and infections. His facial wounds were so extreme that his facial nerve was damaged, causing his upper lip to droop half an inch lower than the other side and allowing drool to escape.

"Harry has spent a week at my house, gradually learning our routine and learning to trust us. He no longer cringes and squints his eyes when we reach to pet him. His tail wags more and more in an ever-widening arc when he greets us. He explores our world and plays a little with some of the dogs. He is even smelling better now that the odour of infection is subsiding.

"Harry greets me now as if I were someone special, and he leans comfortably against my legs. When I sit, he leans against me, gradually lying down to use my feet as a pillow. He comes to me frequently for hugs, and I use a handy paper towel to wipe away the drool. He's not so bony, having gained eight pounds with regular feeding. He loves a belly rub, and he tells me when it is time for one. He sits at my feet, his old dog eyes catching my glance, his tail wagging in response. I hug his still-thin little body and whisper, 'I love ya, Harry,' and I reach for another paper towel to wipe away more drool."

That is what I wrote about Harry, and it was published in our column in the local paper, *The Bugle-Observer* in October 2008. It was accompanied by a picture of Harry with the bloody drainage on his neck and chest in view, supporting hands visible (preventing him from falling). He was in a despicable condition, and I suspected that his life had not been much better—that he was one of those dogs who lived tied to a doghouse in the far corner of a lot. We decided to keep the aged fellow and try to make his last months comfortable and friendly.

Harry was very protective of himself, we found. He could not accept a lift to help him into the car, a nudge to show him which direction he was to go. And he could not be picked up—not without a muzzle. He darted through the opened door when it was time to go outside, looking over his shoulder. (Was he looking for a boot?) He seemed worried if we did anything outside of our established routine. He revelled in a walk in our enclosed field, and he was happily exhausted when we returned to the house. Quickly, he planted himself on the softest of the dog beds and relaxed for a nice nap.

One evening, I encouraged Harry to climb into my lap for some hugs. An attempt to lift him elicited a growl, but when allowed to climb up himself, he relaxed, licked my face, and settled in comfortably for the long term. It became our habit. I would invite him into my lap, and despite the difficulties in getting there, he would not accept help. He was never as happy as when lying in my lap, poking me with his nose if I forgot to continue with the shoulder massage, the ear rubs, or the tummy rubs. His eyes sparkled, and he would look at me with such happiness and contentment that I forgave him the awkwardness of my position and the long periods that I had to maintain it. Finally, reluctantly, he would get down to follow the group outside for a bathroom break while I took my Tylenol.

Harry was such a loving little guy. He seemed to need to be touching us whenever possible. Knowing his time was short, we allowed him to sleep at the foot of our bed, which he loved. The problem, of course, was getting him up onto it. Our technique: throw a towel over his head and quickly lift him and drop him on the bed. The roars, initially accompanied by snapping at us, gradually decreased, but they never really disappeared. We called him "the ingrate" as he snuggled by our legs, perhaps achieving a closeness that he had needed his entire life.

About a month after he joined us, Harry jumped off the bed in the middle of the night and began pacing around the room and panting. Then he threw himself at the low-set bedroom window, and began clawing at the bedroom door. Thinking that he needed to go out, Larry let him out into the pen off our living room and watched as Harry paced back and forth, panting, eyes glazed. Inside, he could not settle and became aggressive if forced to stop. By morning, he was himself again—sweet and cuddly—providing he could walk with the other dogs and rest on his favourite bed. A health assessment, complete with screening blood work, revealed a potential problem with some of his teeth, and that was addressed.

After that, Harry had occasional episodes when he was confused, agitated, and restless. Shannon called him Harold during those periods. My comments to her at work would be, "Harold was here last night," or "I haven't seen Harold for a long time." We consulted many times about his problems, and we treated him with several drugs to try to keep his dementia at bay.

At home, it was tense. We both loved the old dog, and when he was Harry, we enjoyed his company immensely. We wanted to give him all the love and care that we feared he had missed in his previous life. We wanted to coddle him—and yet, we needed our sleep. Some nights, regardless of the dose of medication, Harold would pace, scratch, pant, throw himself at the windows, knock over furniture, and pace back and forth on the back of the sofa. Those nights gradually became more and more frequent. I enjoyed every moment that Harry would sit with me, welcoming him at his whim. I could tell, though, that his personality was deteriorating more and more. Even while sitting on my lap, he would growl if I tried to shift his position.

I recall one evening sitting across from Larry, Harry on my lap, gradually sliding off. Tensions were running high, and Larry said to me, sounding somewhat annoyed, "Help him up, he's sliding onto the floor!" Annoyed myself, I snapped, "When I try to help him, Harold comes!" As we stared at each other, we couldn't help but smile.

Harold came more and more often, and then he began staying most of the day as well. We could keep Harold at bay for short periods with increases in medication, but eventually Harry was so sedated and incapacitated by the medications that we felt we had to let them both go. Reluctantly—and with the help of our good friend,

Shannon—we helped them along. Harold went first, and then a very sleepy Harry went. He knew that we all loved him (and he had finally experienced a short period of the good life that he should have enjoyed all his life).

Chapter 15—Sunday Mornings, Sayin' "Down"

W e meet so many nice animals through the DunRoamin' Stray and Rescue. It's hard to find foster homes for big dogs, so Shannon and I usually do that little chore. Since some of my dogs have homicidal tendencies toward cats (or would that be *felicidal?*), she usually has more cats and I usually have a lot of dogs. My average is around ten large dogs—some strays, many permanent.

It's not that I think they are ungrateful or wilfully inconsiderate, but just once, one Sunday morning, what if I didn't have to get up until, say, 8:30 a.m.? I could do that, probably, if we kennelled each of the dogs in another room or put them in the basement runs, but that would defeat our purpose. The whole premise of having them loose in our home is to teach them how to be good, adoptable pets—they need to learn manners. That makes them highly adoptable.

Still, each morning, the first sound that pierces my consciousness is the "tick, tick, tick, tick, tick, tick!" of the nails of our ancient white dog pacing on the laminate floor of our room. She always gets up at 6:30 a.m. and seems to cry, "Andi want food!" Soon I hear a chuff sound, which escalates to two sharp barks separated by about forty-five seconds. This can continue interminably—or until one of us gets up.

I was supposed to euthanize her about 13 years ago (a stray from animal control, no options for her due to disinterest and overcrowding). It is mornings like this that I question my altruism. I tried to trim her nails yesterday (maybe if they were shorter, I could sleep until she starts barking), but in her confusion and stress, she bit me. That tooth really hurt, and it left a mark on my hand! No sense telling her she's bad or to go back to bed. She's been deaf for two years now. We used to be able to point our index fingers at her as if we were telling her off, and she would stop. Now she refuses to look at us. And with her aged eyes, I'm not convinced she could see enough to understand, anyway. With Andi no longer interactive, we have little recourse but to try to ignore the clicking.

I'm pretty good at that now, but invariably, she steps on Ray, causing him to leap to his feet. He's a big, gentle shepherd mix who was rescued from where he had been abandoned and chained, in the rising waters of a flood plain. Hartland Fire Department heroes took their boat out to rescue the old, starving dog, and he moved in with us. Now Ray joins her pacing, pausing frequently at my face to breathe directly from his 13-year-old open mouth. Now my olfactory senses have been rudely awakened. Ray, regardless of grooming, always looks like an unmade bed.

My feet are toasty warm, so I know that Miles, our Border collie mix, has sneaked into the bed again. He usually does that about 5 a.m., and I feel his head resting on my leg. I love that dog. He was rescued from the trunk of a car at six weeks of age in 35° C weather, and he's my boy. He'd stay in bed all day without a sound, but darn, I hear a subtle tearing sound. That would be Spike, a one-year-old shepherd mix—and that would be bed number five. He gets restless when he's awake and no one wants to get up. Next, he'll put his front paws on the bed and nudge me with his nose. And then, if no one gets up, the destruction will begin. I should have my new glasses next week.

Still, foolishly trying to salvage the morning, I feign sleep until Seven, our Siberian husky, jumps between Larry and me. She was rescued as a puppy from a remote wooded area, critically ill from parvovirus infection. Parvo is a very serious viral illness that is often fatal without intensive treatment. It is very preventable and one of the main reasons we so strongly recommend that people start their pup's vaccinations at eight weeks of age. Leaning heavily on my shoulder, she twists to begin her morning ablutions. In self-defence, I am now forced to cover my head with blankets to avoid morning kisses. (I know where that tongue was just seconds ago!)

Mick, our older collie mix, scraped off the road after being shot about eight years ago, gives a resounding, "Back off!" kind of growl from under the left side of the bed. Someone has stepped on his great plume of a tail or invaded his personal space.

Benton, the new rescue Border collie mix, shyly peaks out from the right side of the bed to see if food might be forthcoming.

Well, hell! Might as well get up! No more sleep for me, anyway. I struggle out of bed, trying to maintain my balance while the seven of us try to pass through the bedroom door simultaneously. Toenails press painfully and repeatedly on the tops of my bare feet. They're going to leave marks!

Politely, Benton, who has slept under the right side of the bed, walks behind us, not participating in the jostling. The muttering pack got what they wanted (me out of bed), and they rush to the door to be let out into the large pen for bathroom duties. Smiling appreciatively, I return Benton's gentlemanly greeting, and he follows the rest outside. He's doing well for a dog who has never been outside except for bathroom duties, never been leashed, never been in a car. He spent his whole life in a small house with his elderly owner. I am amazed at how well he has adjusted to the rat race here.

I slam the door quickly behind the pack, and shivering, I start quickly toward the bedroom but I am stopped by a faint whine. Oops, did I forget Bart? He chose a spot in the living room when he first came here, and he has maintained it ever since. I make a 90-degree turn and stumble, shivering, to help Bart to his feet. Partly due to age—but probably more due to the severe beating the little dog suffered at the hands of his owner before being thrown into the street—Bart often needs help to stand. Ignoring the ungrateful snarl as I help him up (he's due for more pain medications), I watch him hobble to the door and head outside with dignity and determination. He's so old and so sore (his bones were broken during the beating), but he stumbles along, trying to catch up to Benton, whom he really likes.

We're up. All except Easy, Freeman, and Loup. Larry will take care of them. They refuse to join the pack, and they have varying degrees of aggressiveness. Freeman and Loup will eat together. Loup, a large shepherd/malamute cross will attack other dogs, but not Freeman. This I find totally incomprehensible given Freeman's attitude and behaviour (and the fact that I often want to attack Freeman myself!). But they have been kennel mates for years. Loup is the most beautiful, big, brindle husky-like dog. She came here eight years ago, having been shot twice in the chest. She's so good with people, and she loves children but she's not a dog person. Freeman is—well, he's beautiful too, really ... but he's still Freeman.

111

And Easy? She's hard. She came here as a young black pup, attacked by a pack of dogs. She's been adopted out several times. The first return was because she was starting to look like she was a Staffordshire terrier, not what the family wanted. We have her back again. This is the fifth time we've taken her in. I guess she'll stay. She's a great dog, she's just hard-headed and selective regarding her dog friends. If it were up to Easy, I could sleep in as long as I wanted, and she'd keep my back warm. But it would just be Easy and me in the room—no dogs allowed. Therefore, she sleeps in her crate just outside our bedroom door ... with the pack, but not.

We're up, the dogs are fed, and I start breakfast: cereal and a nice hot cup of tea. I settle in to enjoy a bit of *Canada AM*—but wait! Where are the dogs? A quick search finds Seven and Miles in my bed; Mick, Benton, and Spike on the dog beds in the living room; Andi on the bed in the office; Bart back in his bed. And they're all sleeping! Easy naps in her crate.

Various plans for revenge float through my mind, each more diabolical and satisfying than the previous one—some quite clever, actually. And then Mick saunters over, catches my eye, and rests his head on my knee.

"It's okay, you guys," I whisper as I stroke his blond head, "I live to serve."

Chapter 16—Larry the Cat

Upon my return to my hometown to start my own practice, I found a spot on my family's farm that was surrounded on three sides by pasture and not far from the farmhouse and barns. There, I set up my clinic.

This gave me some familiarity with the animal life at the farm, and shortly after settling in, I noted one animal who stood out. He was interesting, intriguing, and different—sort of dangerous, even. His name was Larry the Cat (as opposed to Larry, my husband).

He was legendary for his exploits, his behaviour, his attitude, and his fearlessness. Pugnacious, arrogant, and rude, Larry could easily have been named Attila the Hunter. I treated many a male cat for abscesses, which, I am sure, originated on the points of Larry's claws. Thus, it was with some surprise that I found myself greatly saddened when Larry passed on (in what was at least his 13th year). Further surprising myself, I wrote his obituary in our local newspaper column, "We're All DunRoamin'." Here it is:

He Did It His Way

Larry the barn cat died today, yet another victim of the skin cancer common in white outdoor cats. He will be greatly missed, having been a notable presence on the farm for some 12 years. The intensity of the feeling of loss (or its presence itself) is likely to be species specific—the greatest loss is felt by his human friends. Some farm residents will feel only a profound sense of relief. Found in the back, wooded section of the farm, he was initially called Lurleen, but when his health care included a neuter, his name was changed to Larry. His most notable feature was attitude—a complete indifference to social norms, a lack of gratitude for a good meal, and no need for personal validation.

Larry became an institution at the farm—a rather volatile, unpredictable, potentially violent, somehow admirable, sociopathic institution. If he had a soft, warm, fuzzy side, it was seen only by his closest friends. He was what he was—no apologies.

If memory serves, Larry expelled many itinerant male cats from the main barns, including (but not limited to) Achilles, Snarles, Casper, Bathurst, Fraidy, and Blues. Why he allowed Hamish and Argyle, two neutered male cats, to live in his domain defies explanation. Even the dogs stepped respectfully around him.

Larry's white coat was rarely pristine, and he was frequently scarred and bloody from fights with the house cats and neighbours' cats. Hungry, he would greet you with fond hellos and purrs, rubbing affectionately around your ankles. Fed, he would slap and hiss if he was petted too many times, or if your technique was not to his liking. Refusing to be anyone's house cat, he would sneak into whichever house appealed to him at the moment, grab a quick snack (be it cat food or food from the kitchen counter), enjoy a short nap, and then be gone.

His domain extended to the neighbouring fields in all directions, his white coat a beacon as he patrolled his kingdom. He was a crackerjack ratter and a mouser beyond belief. The spoils of his hunts were often displayed prominently around the barnyard, a warning to all.

Nothing frightened Larry, and many a dog gained a healthy respect for cats thanks to Larry. I remember our foxhound, Dusty, racing toward me, eyes wide with fright. Larry was literally on his tail, hissing and slashing. His ego was so large that, one night, Larry had to be forcibly removed from the clinic steps when he refused to allow a client and his large dog to enter the building.

My favourite image of Larry, though, is of him sitting on the top of a fence post, idly grooming his paws. As I watched, the horse walked slowly toward him and inquisitively extended her nose to sniff him—and went flying backward! Larry's slashing claws had left bleeding criss-crossed scratches on her soft, velvety nose. And Larry? He finished his ablutions, sublimely unaffected by the encounter.

Larry scratched everyone, fussed at everyone, and used and abused everyone. He made us laugh, made us angry, and made us bleed—often in the same sixty seconds. If he allowed us to pet him, we felt honoured. If he scratched us, we felt that we knew better than to bother him. Acquaintances were at most risk, his responses to them unpredictable. He sometimes allowed his few close friends to hold him for short periods, and he even deigned to purr for a select, flattered few.

As I write, I notice, from the corner of my eye, my right index fingernail, still purple from my most recent attempt to bring Larry into the clinic for treatment. The other bite wounds and multiple scratches to my hands and arms (now almost healed with some noticeable scarring) forced me to release Larry and dashed any hopes I had of attempting palliative care for his disease. He died as he lived—independent, uncompromising, determined, hateful, self-absorbed, admired, respected, known by many, friend to few.

If Frank Sinatra ever needed the living essence of his famous song, "I Did It My Way," it was Larry the Cat. We'll miss him.

Chapter 17—It Can Be Done; It's Easy

The first time I met her, she was dropped off at the clinic, a four- or five-month-old black pup found on the road with multiple deep and infected bite wounds obvious. Her benefactor was not interested in adopting or fostering her, so after she was treated, vaccinated, and cleaned up, I called Larry to take her to our home.

Much later, during a short lull in appointments, I called home to ask, "How is she?" I meant, "Does she get along with our other dogs? Is she fearful? How is her temperament?" His answer was, "Oh, she's easy." She was easy—for two or three weeks as she recovered from the toll taken by living as a stray. She loved people and certain dogs, and she was very hard-headed. As she recovered from her ordeal, it was obvious that she had a mind of her own ... and no tolerance for a lack of dog manners. Easy was adopted at about six or seven months (by that point, a large black dog who loved the children and the family's other dog).

A few months later, she was returned. The return wasn't due to behaviour issues, it was because she was changing in appearance, and people were asking whether she was a pit bull. The wife was not interested in having that breed of dog in her home with her children. In fact, the husband and children were devastated to lose her, but the mother's deeply ingrained fear of the pit bull and its reputation for attacking persuaded them to give her up.

Admittedly, she had developed the muscled, sleek body and head of the Staffordshire terrier with just a hint of lab. She was built like the proverbial brick outhouse.

Still, her great temperament, her love of life, her playfulness, and her complete trust in us won us over again. Yes, she didn't like Mick or Miles (the collie types), but she would play endlessly with any dog who didn't belong to us. She wasn't vicious, but she could be aggressive—especially with our dogs. It was with shame and embarrassment, though, that we watched the 14-year-old arthritic lab mix visiting our neighbour chase a terrified Easy back onto our property. We would have been horrified if she had fought. She's not allowed out of our yard, and she had no business visiting our neighbour's house, but still.

Easy had a very strong aversion to being confined. We had originally left her loose in the house when we were out, but we found that she was climbing on our counters in search of interesting little tidbits: pens, bread, medications. And she had been taking the oestrogen pills intended for another dog's leaky bladder—as if she needed oestrogen on board with that attitude! She also found and ingested arthritis medication for our old dogs, antibiotics for one with a urinary tract infection, several rolls of Tums, five pens, two birthday cards (intended for me), a nice pair of black leather gloves, and several sticky notes reminding Larry of his dental appointments and chores that needed to be done. All were, we thought, safely on the counter. We decided to kennel her when out, and we left her in a large plastic Vari-Kennel the next day. Upon our return, she met us at the door, more oestrogen pills eaten, Vari-Kennel partially apart, door ajar. "We'll try the wire crates," we said. Same result: she happily greeted us at the door. The rooms were a shambles, and there were bite wounds on one of the old dogs.

We thought, *Okay, no one hurts the oldies! Let's put her in the run in the basement when we're out.* She was still there when we returned, but the wire was badly bent around the door, and one of her canine teeth was broken. There was also evidence that she had spent some time and energy at the back where the run abuts the wall—wood chips, bent wire, and two loosened nails attested to her determination.

By the time Easy was two years old, we had used and discarded all the confinement systems at our house. She did not demonstrate signs of separation anxiety; she was just determined that she would not be confined in an area that she did not like. She easily scaled the six-foot fences of the runs and escaped. She dug holes under the fences and escaped. She chewed through rope, clothesline, and light chains. She broke collars. She leapt from the top of doghouses onto eight-foot fences and escaped. We were afraid that she would be hit by a car or that our neighbours might complain if she decided to fight with their dogs.

Finally, we built Easy's Run, a four-foot by eight-foot run on a thick wooden base with heavy support pipes. Wire was securely fastened over the top and tied to the frame at three-inch intervals. Easy hated it until we took it all apart and added a doghouse for her. Still, she would not do any bathroom duties in the run, requiring us to drive home at noon to let her out.

Elated at our success in safely confining her in our absence, we relaxed and allowed her to play in our yard with more and more freedom. A short time later, ignoring our commands to return to us, she went for an adventure. When she was found a half-hour later, she happily accepted a drive home. She would escape the minute our backs were turned or from the confines of the field or anywhere in our yard, but she was always happy to accept a drive home.

She was then adopted into a family whose entire house and yard were set up for dogs. Believing in full disclosure, we chronicled her list of misdemeanours while her new family laughed and hugged her.

Updates from them included her escapes, their unhappy neighbours (they didn't want dogs on their lawn), and endearing stories about her personality and hysterical behaviours.

Then Easy and one of their other dogs, a female, came into the clinic as emergencies. Easy's escapes had become so frequent (with neighbourly threats to shoot her), it had forced them to try an electric fence inside their run (similar to the one Larry and I had tried years ago). It worked, too, for a while—until Easy got a shock trying to escape, blamed it on the dog standing next to her, and started the mother of all fights. That was forgiven and the sutured wounds healed, but Easy never forgot the cause of her shock. Soon, she and the other dog were fighting constantly. As per our agreement, if they could not keep her, she was to be returned to us.

Although she had been gone almost a year, her run was still intact (having been home to a stray dog who whelped her litter just twenty-four hours after moving in and various other strays). A thorough check and repair of any perceived weaknesses in the run was completed, and Easy moved back in. By now, three canine teeth were fractured. I assumed they were hurting her, so we had them removed. This resulted in a bright-eyed, alert, responsive, mischievous, and hard-headed dog whose tongue often fell out one side of her mouth (giving her a very quirky Staffordshire terrier look). She often retraced her steps to pick up the ball that frequently would pop out of her mouth while playing fetch. Toys, even flat Nylabones, were difficult to pick up without her canine teeth, but that only increased her interest in them and her determination to have them.

Then a young woman fell in love with her and became determined to have her. A great long list of instructions was given, including who was to enter or leave a room first, where Easy was to walk, how to anticipate and stop Easy's outbursts at other dogs, etc. These instructions came from spending many hours training with her. Uncharacteristically (and contrary to my worries), Easy howled all night and was returned the next day. It was like she had never been gone. Months later, a trucker and his wife came to meet Easy. They fell for her immediately—again, despite full disclosure. Easy would sit in the car all day. She loved car rides. It seemed ideal to ride with a trucker, one on one, always going down the road.

A few months later, she and her family dropped by our house. They were returning Easy. Apparently, she was going through window screens and screened doors to go for a run (but she'd always return). Also, she had escaped from the truck when left with the window down.

By this time, Easy's run was gone, replaced by a garage with one bay heated for the dog-loathing Freeman and Loup (but mostly for Larry's Harley Davidson motorcycle).

"Okay," we said, "we'll make a run in the garage." We built an eight-foot by four-foot by eight-foot enclosure on the cement floor with wire over the top. Later, I said, "All finished! We'll only be gone an hour." When we returned, I said, "How did she move that run all the way across the garage to within inches of the Harley?!" Larry's face had turned white when he saw its proximity to the bike. Now, when we are asked why the run is spiked to the wall, we simply reply, "It's Easy's."

I get a Dr. Seuss kind of feeling when I think of Easy's aversion to confinement. Here's something I came up with:

> I do not like to be confined,
> Not in a cage, not in my mind.
> I do not like it in a crate,
> Not in a cage, I'm in a rage.
> Not with a gauge,
> Not for a wage.
> I will not stay within a pen—
> Not in the sun,
> It won't be done.
> I will not stay within a house—
> Not with a mouse.
> I will not stay there with a spouse,
> Or even Faust.
>
> Will I stay in with a man?
> I doubt I can, unless I'm a fan!
> Does he have a van?
>
> Okay, I'll try it with a guy!
> Oh my, oh my, the time does fly!
> Yes, I like it with a guy,
> I'd like to stay, not run away.
> I think it's settled,

Yes, okay.
In a house or in a run,
But with the guy, not on the fly—
And by and by, if I don't cry,
And can convince him he's my guy,
(That's not a lie)
Then I'll start to wonder why
I used to like it on the lam.
I did not like the door to slam,
But now he shares his eggs and ham.
And I'm his dog now,
Yes, I am!

That's Easy. She has become a much better-behaved dog. She doesn't run away or dive through screens. She has the occasional scrap with the other residents here, but damage is much less severe since she had the three broken canine teeth (fangs) removed. Still, she bears watching. I think our friend Brian said it best when he commented, "You should have named her Hard!"

That Easy! She's a riot! She loves to nap with me, cuddling up close and answering all my questions. "How's that, Easy?" "*Mmm!*" "Am I hugging you too tight?" "*Rrr!*" "Tired?" "*Mmm.*" "Are you a pit?" "*Rrr!*" Larry says that, when we go for a nap, it's nothing but a pit-y party.

Chapter 18—Bedtime

We have a routine in the evenings at our house. Shortly after 9 p.m., with nine dogs sound asleep on the living room floor and Easy asleep in her crate, I stand up and say, "Well …" The permanent residents immediately jump to their feet and run to the door to go outside, followed more slowly by the foster dogs.

Right now, three of them are fosters. One of them, Spike, is a young shepherd/Doberman mix. He is quite a handful; he was completely untrained when he came to us. He has been with us for six months, and we find him to be very sweet. Though he's still a pup, he has eyes that shine with goodness and intelligence. He'll be a fine dog when he grows up. He knows the drill, but he is careful to display proper manners when around the older dogs.

The second foster is Harvey. He was discarded when he was found to be very ill with a preventable parvovirus infection at eight months of age. DunRoamin' sponsored him, treated his disease, and paid for the treatment. He's fine now. A short-haired boxer mix, he has eyes that can look right into your soul. He's a cuddle pup—a 40-pound lap setter—and he is never as happy as when he is close to you. He plays well with the other two fosters.

The third is Nigel. He's also eight months old, weighs about 80 pounds, and has been confined to a crate for six weeks while his casted broken hind leg heals. He's a lab/shepherd mixed with something big and black. He's also a bull-in-a-china-shop kind of dog. If it's in the way, he goes through it or knocks it over. I can't blame him for his enthusiasm because it appears he was living outdoors with very little human contact until he came to DunRoamin'. Now, having become used to the sounds and routines of the house (and having gotten his cast off last week), he is doing really well. Had I known him better when he arrived, I think that I would have called him Moose. I don't think there's any dog or any thing in our living room that he hasn't knocked over yet, including me. I keep thinking that this uncontrolled enthusiasm, this excitement at being allowed to be loose and out of his crate, will eventually wane. But so far, no luck. Still, Nigel is a good fellow, and although he thinks the world is one big game, he's learning a few manners—albeit slowly!

With this background, let me tell you about bedtime the other night. Nine dogs dash outside for duties, and then eight dogs accompany me into our tiny bathroom, jostling me as I try to take my medication, pouncing on anything that lands on the floor. Pauper—a very old, short-legged rescue dog found wandering the streets of a nearby city in bone-chilling weather—stays with Larry. Larry drove to the shelter, which was very frightening for poor old Pauper, and he brought him home to live out his last months with us. He has been Pauper's hero ever since, and the little dog spends every minute that he can sitting with Larry and leaning on his leg.

I shuffle my way to the toilet. Multiple canine feet tread painfully on my feet, and we all gather around the flush. I snatch the toilet paper from its holder, having repeatedly told our housekeeper to leave it on the high windowsill because Mick, the collie mix, eats it. Finished, the nine of us watch in fascination as the water swirls in the toilet bowl, and I immediately close its cover. Drinking water is in the kitchen.

My entourage then moves with me to the bedroom. Miles, my Border collie buddy and permanent shadow since he was rescued from the sweltering trunk of a car when he was six weeks old, immediately jumps in the centre of the bed. Old Mick, who has stopped acknowledging any foster dogs at all for the past few years, takes his place under the bed, tail visible if I look down over the edge. Seven, the lovely blue-eyed husky, jumps onto the bed at shoulder level, rests her head there, and looks at me with such undying love and devotion in her eyes. I am not fooled. I recognize her expression of love for the outright lie that it is, but I smile because I appreciate the effort anyway. She would leave with the first person who asked her and never look back. I've seen her do it—more than once.

Forgetting protocol and just needing a hug, Harvey (the young boxer mix) takes a huge leap and lands precariously between Seven and Miles. Glancing at their hostile stares, he immediately realizes his mistake but is at a loss as to how to correct it. After a hard glare and a low growl, Miles relaxes. Seven, who hates crowding, leaves the bed—vacating the perfect spot for Harvey to cuddle without disturbing Miles.

And Spike? He's on the best bed on the floor, curled into a tight ball, blinking at me through sleepy eyes. I love him when he's tired. He's so sweet. And ancient Andi, she's lying adjacent to Spike, clearly down for the night. (Early to bed, early to rise!)

I smile. They're all so good. And then Nigel comes flying into the room, oozing mischief and stored energy. Shannon, who looks after all our orthopaedic cases, would be horrified to know (and I'd be in big trouble if she did know), but Nigel launched his 80-pound body through the air and onto our elevated bed. He landed on the centre puppy, 40-pound Harvey, and caused Miles to leap to his feet and threaten to tear him limb from limb. Now, I know (but Nigel doesn't) that Miles is all show, but this is a good one. And Nigel, having landed on Harvey and afraid to move, does what any good submissive pup does: he lies down in the presence of his betters.

Mick is now tired of the pups' uproar, and he is roaring obscenities from under the bed—he even woke up Andi. I'm worried about Harvey because I can't see his head and know he won't move in the face of Miles's tirade. I wonder whether he can breathe under Nigel's weight. Only his hind legs are visible, extending perpendicularly to Nigel's stomach.

A sharp word from me, and Miles ends his roaring. Mick, however, continues. With all my strength, I push Nigel onto the left side of the bed, leaving Harvey freed, and thankfully, breathing normally. Andi is on her feet, and in her wobbly gait, she walks in small circles around her bed, confused and intermittently stepping on Mick's tail (resulting in further shouts of outrage from him).

I get up, settle Andi, push Mick's tail farther under the bed, and following a brief but enthusiastic wrestling match with Nigel, manage to get him onto Larry's side of the bed so I can get back in.

Finally, Larry's curiosity gets the better of him, and he enters the room to see Nigel, still in play mode, on the bed and chewing on Harvey's now wet and saliva-covered head.

"I'll take him with me," he says, and he starts out of the room with Nigel by the collar. Surreptitiously, I assess the gait in Nigel's rear leg, and I can't see any marked change. Thank goodness for that.

Troublemaker gone, Miles, Harvey, and I start to drift off to sleep, and then, vaguely, I hear Larry climbing into bed.

"Oh, God!" he exclaims loudly and with great disgust.

"What's wrong?" I mumble sleepily.

"There are anal gland secretions on my pillow case!" Anal glands are small sacs on both sides of a dog's anus that secrete very foul-smelling secretions, usually when the dog moves its bowels. A sudden fright, however, can cause them to be emptied. I hear Larry swearing as he strips the covering from both of his pillows and stomps to the linen closet for clean pillowcases. That must have scared Nigel more than I thought!

"I didn't do it!" I exclaim as he again climbs into bed. *Nothing he can say to dispute that fact,* I think as I drift off to sleep.

In fitting with convention, Miles and Harvey slide off the foot of the bed and seek out one of the many dog beds on the floor. I think, *What's the big deal? I still can't smell any anal glands,* but I let it go. No sense poking a tiger in the eye.

Chapter 19—Conversations

Our contact with the public, especially in the wee hours of the morning, has opened many a veterinarian's eyes to the diversity of human behaviours and perspectives. Many of these conversations were memorable, but more were hilarious. A classmate of mine, Lynn, received an excited phone call from someone named Marvin in the middle of the night during our internship in Saskatoon. In an excited, nearly panicky voice, he blurted, "Umm, umm, my cat just had, like, a kitten, and, you know, like, you won't believe this, but like, well, her *liver* came right out behind it!" Struggling against her urge to chuckle, the vet replied, "Well, Marvin, pretty sure that's not her liver!" before going on to explain about placentas and afterbirth. The kitten, while in its mother's womb, is nourished by a very vascular organ connecting the kitten to its mothers blood supply. It is expelled after the kitten is born because it is no longer needed after birth. It is purplish (as the liver often is), and it was easy to see how he could become confused. Still, if he thought that his cat was in trouble, it was better to have called for help than to wait until it was too late.

Stories abound about middle-of-the-night phone calls. One such call from an older gentleman informed me of a six-month-old cat that was down on its side and unable to get up. The caller asked me to come to his house. I replied that it would be much better if he brought the cat to the clinic where all my drugs and equipment were available. "How would I bring it in?" he asked hesitantly. Patiently, I replied that he should just put it in the car and drive it to my clinic. In the intervening silence—and aware of the frigid temperatures that night—I added that because it was so cold, he should wrap it in a blanket or put it in his coat for warmth. "Inside my jacket?" he squeaked incredulously. "Yes!" I responded somewhat testily. "Next to your body so he stays warm!" I'd had my fill of those people who felt that cats were meant to live outside, surviving and sustaining themselves by catching mice. I knew how hard and short the lives of those cats were. It made me furious when people felt that a cat's life had no value because they could easily replace it with another free cat. I was surprised that he had even bothered to call me given his apparent attitude.

"How would I do that?" he again questioned uncertainly.

"Just tuck the thing in your jacket and drive here!" I responded shortly, already tired of this nocturnal conversation and concerned about the mental health of my caller.

Slowly, he remarked, "My other vet always came to the farm."

"Well, I—" I started indignantly, and then I stopped abruptly. *Farm?*

"Did you say cat or calf?" I asked sheepishly while a mental image of the gentleman driving his car with a 600-pound calf in his jacket caused a giggle to escape.

"It's a six-month-old calf," he replied patiently.

"You'll want the large animal vet, then," I told him, still giggling. "I thought you said cat! You have the small animal clinic! I'll give you the number of the large animal vet." I was still giggling, and I was very pleased when I heard his chuckle.

Other office conversations can be just as tricky. When seeing a young client and her large breed dog in the office one day, she remarked that she really wanted to adopt another dog, but that her fiancé had told her that no one has more than one large dog in a house. "But just yesterday, in the Sobey's parking lot, I saw someone with five big dogs in a grey Toyota, and they all seemed fine!"

"Well," I answered slowly, "I don't think that I am the best one to advise you on that, but—" and she interrupted me with, "But you're the vet! If you can't help me, who can? You should know if it's okay to have two big dogs together in one household!" As she stopped for breath, I quickly inserted, "Yes, but I was the one in the Toyota!"

On another day, I led a sobbing, distraught woman into the exam room, gently disengaging her fingers from an old blue cat carrier. Piecing together her story through her sobs and hand wringing, I concluded that she believed that someone in her community—a cat hater—was kidnapping cats and abandoning them in the forest outside of her town. Her beloved cat had disappeared as well as those of many of her neighbours. She had just found her cat on the roadside as she was driving through the wooded area, her long-missing Precious—finally returned to her.

"It doesn't even look like Precious!" she wailed. "Poor thing! She's lost weight, and she's so matted! I can't stand what has happened to her!" Wretchedly, she watched me examine the poor animal, reaching out frequently to caress the head of the thin, purring cat while tears slid from her reddened eyes. To my dismay, my physical exam revealed an insurmountable flaw in her story. This could not be the lovely Precious that she knew! This was an un-neutered tom, very well endowed for his size. When gently informed of his anatomical parts, she abruptly stood and left the room. "Well then," she said, "I don't want the stupid thing!" Suppressing a grin, I thought, *Well, I do!*" I said to the cat, "Want to stay here until we get you all cleaned up and neutered, Purrley?"

I love those big toms with the big cheeks and grizzled good looks. For the most part, we've found that, after being neutered and becoming used to living indoors, very few want to resume their outdoor life. They find home life a luxurious relief to the daily struggles involved with surviving outdoors.

In our area, there have been several spots where many outdoor cats have disappeared, never to be seen again. The problem is usually an influx of wild predators—pushed by our encroachment on their territories—into more urban areas. There, they find our uninitiated pets to be easy pickings. Foxes, coyotes, bobcats, and some birds of prey feast on our pets. That hunting resulted in our clinic advising owners to keep their small pets indoors or to build covered cat runs for them. Add on the dangers from dogs, cars, poisonings, and cruel people—and life can be very dangerous for an outdoor cat.

These conversations with clients are so intriguing, and I never know where an inquiry will lead. Take this story, for example. I still get a warm, fuzzy feeling whenever I think of this one. A gentleman brought his big lug of a dog in for an examination and vaccines. We call all the lab types *labradogs,* and this one was a beauty: very large, shiny, and black with the kindest, most intelligent eyes that I think I have ever seen. As I questioned him about his dog's medical history, he admitted that he knew very little about the dog's past.

He told me that he and his family had finally decided that the time was right to get a puppy. His two daughters and their parents had agreed, unanimously, to get a puppy (not an older dog) because the children wanted to enjoy watching the pup grow. They went to a local shelter to see the available pups, and they stopped to say hello to the big black dog who wagged his tail in friendly greeting and gazed at them with the kindest eyes. As they started to look at puppies, a passing shelter worker told them that the dog had been there a very long time, and no one was interested in adopting him. He was slated to be put down the next day. The family held an emergency meeting and unanimously agreed, without hesitation, to adopt the dog. "How are things working out for you?" I asked. Looking affectionately down at the big dog, he smiled and said, "He fits in great with our family. He already knows all the girls' secrets, but he's not talking!" There's nothing like a big bear of a dog for a confidant. He will never breathe a word that has been shared with him—guaranteed!

Another take on animal associations came to light for me when a local minister brought a large, very rough-looking stray tom cat in for an examination and treatment of a very large abscess. As I commended him for his concern for the animal's welfare and his desire to help the cat, he said with a grin, "Well, I didn't know if this was a test, and I certainly didn't want to fail if it was!" People's minds are so interesting, and I smiled as this man left with the stray. In my mind, he had passed the "test" with flying colours, and he had promised to be the benefactor and protector of one of God's needy creatures—a fine man, in my estimation.

And finally, under the conversation subtitle of "Never assume anything," one of our clients dropped into the clinic to pick up a prescription cat food diet for his neutered male cat. The very heavy male cat had had severe recurrent episodes of urinary tract blockage, a condition in which crystals build up in the bladder of susceptible cats and result in a blockage of the urethra (the tube that empties the bladder to the outside). This blockage can result in death if left untreated, and it certainly can be costly to treat repeatedly. I was adamant that the cat stay on the prescription food for the rest of his life to prevent further blockage because he had just had a recent episode. I also had instructed the owner to keep his cat indoors for several weeks in order to monitor for any further problems. I didn't want him outdoors, blocked, and unable to receive help.

I said to his owner as I passed him in the waiting room, "How's he doing?"

He replied, "Oh, he gets out today!"

That couldn't be right, I thought, *I just discharged him a few days ago!*

I questioned, "You're letting him out?"

"Yes," he answered, "they said he could go."

Sometimes, I find, clients will take direction from someone who has had dogs all his life or the cat guy down the road rather than taking medical advice from me. Feeling my frustration rise, I asked, "Who said he could?"

"His doctors did!" my client replied.

I stared at him for a moment before asking, "Who are we talking about, Eddie?"

"My brother!" he answered. "They're letting him out of the hospital!"

"Oh," I responded slowly and with a confounded smile, "I'm talking about your cat!"

When he left, we were in total agreement: the cat would stay in, his brother would get out!

Finally, I must relate to you a story about a young child who came to my house with his parents to meet my dogs and foster dogs. As he asked about each individual in my dog area, I told him of each dog's background and the adversity that each had overcome to reach DunRoamin' and be ready to become a family pet. "That dog is Mick. He was found lying on the side of the road. Someone had shot him. But he's all right now." "That's Havoc. His owner was going to shoot him because it costs too much to feed him." "That's Stanley. He was abandoned in the mountains the night of the Stanley Cup. We call him the Stanley Pup." "That's Nigel. His owner wanted to euthanize him because he was unable to afford to fix his broken leg." "That's Miles. He was brought to us with heat stroke because his owner had put him in the trunk of the car on a very hot day. A young boy heard him crying and asked if he could have him. He knew his family could not keep him, but he also knew how wrong the treatment was." "That's Maggie. Her family wanted to kill her rather than pay to have the porcupine quills removed." "They are all right now." As I finished my litany of stories, the youngster looked at me and—completely missing my point in telling him the stories—said, "Wow! You must be a really good person!"

Well, I'm not—but I hate injustice, cruelty, and suffering. I love the little critters that depend on us for a good life. I feel an affinity for them—and I half believe my sister's statement that they are angels, sent here to teach us valuable life lessons and make our lives better.

Afterword

If this book has opened your mind to the possibility that animals have very active internal lives, I hope it will be a stepping stone to a full-fledged appreciation of the complexities of the animal psyche. If you already knew that this was the case, I hope this book makes you feel that there is hope for the human race in its dealings with our animal friends. Perhaps it is not that they cannot speak, it's just that we cannot understand their language.

Animal welfare is a very busy arena now, and it's difficult to understand with the complexities of our dietary customs and our use of animals in work situations, entertainment arenas, scientific studies, and in the house as companions. Animal welfare groups speak of the five freedoms that we must allow in our animals. Those basic freedoms are as follows: freedom from hunger and thirst; freedom from discomfort; freedom from pain, injury, or disease; freedom from distress; freedom to express behaviours that promote well-being. That is certainly a valid place to start.

There are many ways to become involved in the rescue, care, and protection of needy animals. Most areas have animal shelters where volunteers are needed to help with animal care and socialization.

We actually have some volunteers who are not physically able to clean and empty litter boxes or scrub the cat rooms. They do a fine job hugging and socializing our cats. The cats love it—as do the volunteers.

If you are able (and have familiarized yourself and your family with the duties and responsibilities attached to being the guardian of a dog or cat or any prospective pet), adopting a needy animal is a great help to the animal and the rescue or shelter. If you can't adopt, perhaps you can volunteer at a shelter or be a fundraiser for that shelter. Animal shelters depend heavily on donated moneys to pay all their bills: vet bills, food bills, rent, utilities, and staff salaries. Perhaps you are able to create websites on which animal photos can be displayed. Maybe your photography skills can be used. Perhaps you are exceptional at creating work schedules. Maybe you can write articles about the shelter animals for the local newspaper. Maybe you can do bookkeeping for the shelter or donate your accounting skills. Maybe you can bake for a bake sale, run bottle drives, or organize talent shows. The list is limited only by your imagination. All these ways of supporting your shelters or rescues result in the care and potential rehoming of needy animals. Could anything better happen to a lonely, frightened dog than to be welcomed into a safe, secure, loving home?

Our group, DunRoamin' Stray and Rescue Inc. has a website through which we try to keep interested supporters up to date on our activities. We report new patients, lost patients, new adoptions, and upcoming events that we are sponsoring. The website, www.dunroaminstrayandrescue.com, also has a PayPal site to promote ease of donations and several contact addresses where questions can be directed. We have a telephone line, which is answered twice daily to receive messages pertinent to the welfare of stray or injured animals.

Also, we have found it prudent to assign an emergency phone to a volunteer so that veterinarians can be reached immediately if strays' or unowned animals' lives are in danger. We are beginning to work more closely with other shelters, both in caring for sick animals and in fundraising. As long as it gets helped, it doesn't matter where the needy animal is or who raised the money. It is *all* about the animals. *Nothing* else!

I have always been a voracious reader, devouring any book on animals—dogs especially—serial killer fictional stories, and thrillers. One book that I first read more than 20 years ago went a long way toward opening my eyes and causing me to think in a different way. It was called *Don Coyote: The Good Times and the Bad Times of a Much Maligned American Original* by Dayton O. Hyde. I still have my battered, dog-eared copy from 1989.

Some of the other books that have influenced my thinking include the following:

Wild and Woolly: Tails from a Woodland Studio by Linda Johns
Animals as Teachers and Healers: True Stories and Reflections by Susan Chernak McElroy
Animals in Translation: Using the Mysteries of Autism to Decode Animal Behaviour by Temple Grandin and Catherine Johnson
Dogtown: Tales of Rescue, Rehabilitation, and Redemption by Stefan Bechtel
Out of Harm's Way: The Extraordinary True Story of One Woman's Lifelong Devotion to Animal Rescue by Terri Crisp and Samantha Glen

There are so many really great books to interest and inspire an animal lover or advocate. You only have to look.